Riding
for the Rest of Us

Riding
for the Rest of Us

A Practical

Guide for

Adult Riders

Jessica Jahiel

Howell Book House
New York

Howell Book House
A Simon & Schuster Macmillan Company
1633 Broadway
New York, NY 10019

MACMILLAN is a registered trademark of Macmillan, Inc.
Library of Congress Cataloging-in-Publication Data

Jahiel, Jessica.
    Riding for the rest of us : a practical guide for adult riders / Jessica Jahiel.
        p.   cm.
    Includes bibliographical references and index.
    ISBN 0-87605-909-4
    1. Horsemanship. I. Title.
    SF309.J365 1996
    798.2—dc20   96-1244
                                  CIP

Manufactured in the United States of America
10 9 8 7 6 5 4 3 2 1

All photographs by Adam Jahiel
Book design by A & D Howell

Contents

Acknowledgments

This book exists because I wanted a book for my students to read. I needed a helpful, useful book, directed at the situations and needs of adult non-professional riders, and I couldn't find exactly what I wanted anywhere. So, for all the students who have said, "I wish I'd known this before" and "I wish you would write a book"—here's the book, and I hope you're happy now. It's for all of you.

The photographs in this book are of real, working adults and their real, sometimes slightly-less-than-perfect horses. My thanks to the photographer, Adam Jahiel, and to the models: Cathe Capel and Clemson; Paige Miller and Nate and Zydecko; Carolyn Pribble and Sundance; Beth Saupe and Topper; Luanne Thulstrup and Greta.

In addition to the photographer and the models, I would like to thank the following people: My parents, Edwin and Lenrose Jahiel, who supported this effort in every way. My colleagues, here and abroad, who encouraged me when I got frustrated and who always had time to compare war stories in letters and in late-night phone calls. Ruth Harvie, who read the outline and said, "You have to write this." David Barneby and Sarah and Victoria Shortridge, for giving me the opportunity to teach in England. Karen Fletcher and Maureen Tan, for revisions, suggestions, and constant encouragement. And, most of all, my students—for asking good questions and demanding real answers.

Foreword

In a perfect world, every one of us would own a stable full of fancy, sound, exquisite horses and have access to quality instruction on a regular basis. We'd have the luxury to pursue our goals free from work, family, or financial constraints. We'd be young, fit, supple, and athletic. We'd be confident in our riding and training abilities and possess the mental skills to focus, block out distractions, and problem-solve unemotionally.

The reality, however, is that few of us live in that equestrian utopia. Most of us fall into the category of the underfit, overly stressed, weekend rider who juggles a family and works full-time to support her passion. Few of us can pursue our sport without restrictions; most of us find the obstacles somewhat daunting and discouraging.

Riding for the Rest of Us addresses these very real issues. Jessica Jahiel has taken her years of experience as a teacher, trainer, horse lover, and student of equine and human nature, and put it all together for us in a reader-friendly, understandable style. This book is filled with practical advice for the average horse lover who struggles with physical, emotional, psychological, and financial shortcomings. Jessica takes those limitations and gives you a new perspective on them. Those perceived drawbacks need not prevent you from enjoying your riding and, in most cases, can be turned into advantages. (There's a lot to be said for the benefits of maturity.) She's a real possibility thinker and will help you find realistic solutions to all your challenges while encouraging you to be an active participant in the problem-solving process.

My first reaction when I read this book is that it actually could have been entitled *Riding for Most of Us*. Even though I've been fortunate enough to have horses in my life as my career for the last twenty-odd years, I felt that Jessica was speaking directly to me. I am the one-horse owner, with more time than money, who usually has to train alone. I rode as a child, took a long break, and returned to horses as an adult. I am one of those with more drive than talent who struggles every day with an uncooperative, often painful body. But most of all, I was one of those individuals who needed to learn to compete only with myself, that winning is highly personal, and that it's the journey as much as the destination that really counts. To echo Jessica's sentiments, I needed to learn that "progress not perfection" is the true measure of success.

My next thought was to ponder how Jessica had managed to get into my head. Somehow she had read my thoughts, discovered my philosophy towards riding and training, and written it all down in a clear, compassionate, and enjoyable way. (Be forewarned: She's very clever at blending in those much-needed life lessons with what appears to be a horse book.)

How did she know how strongly I feel about the importance of attitude? No situation is inherently good or bad. What matters is the way you chose to look at it. Give Jessica any set of conditions, and her approach is that your attitude determines your altitude. No matter what the situation, she ever so gently shows you how to see your "problems" as challenges. For instance, she'll help you to see that it's not what you have that matters; it's what you do with what you have. Having been one of those whose first five years of dressage instruction consisted of four formal lessons per year, I can truly relate to her solutions and practical approaches to real-life riding dilemmas.

No matter who you are, this down-to-earth, insightful text will provide you with a delightful formula for enjoying the time you spend with your equine partner. Take a gallon of practical information, add two cups common sense, a generous amount of humor and empathy, and sprinkle the entire mixture with patience, care, and love of the animal, and you'll have the recipe for *Riding for the Rest of Us*.

Jane Savoie
1992 Olympic Dressage Team Reserve Rider
Author of That Winning Feeling!

Introduction

Who *are* "the rest of us"?

Several years ago, I went out to breakfast one morning with two students who had gotten up early to share a drive to the barn and a six o'clock lesson. As we sat over our coffee, we were talking about horse books and magazines and how helpful they were. Diane pulled a horse magazine from her purse and said "Here, look at this."

One of the articles discussed draw reins. Another one described a wealthy young couple who had built a new riding and training facility. There was a piece about the latest styles in riding coats and breeches, and, finally, an interview with a famous jumping star.

"I like this stuff, it's fun, but I wish I could find something written for *me*. Everything seems to be written for someone like my daughter: she's fifteen, and she's showing every weekend all summer. Or else it's aimed at adults, but they're not like me or my friends; they may be 30-something or 40-something, but they're super-fit, super-rich, and have umpteen horses and ride all the time. What about the rest of us?

"Why isn't there a book for riders like Kathy and me? We have *one* horse each, we work, we have families, we have practically *no* time to do this, we just ride whenever we can, but we want to do it anyway. I want to keep learning about riding, and get better at it, and *not* get hurt—I can't *afford* to get hurt.

"I want to know how to find a good place to keep my horse, and how I can tell whether it's safe. I want to know if I'm working correctly between lessons—and I need to get every single thing I can out of my lessons. I want to know how to talk to the vet so that I don't feel totally ignorant. I want to know how I'm supposed to stay riding-fit when I don't get to ride at all for a week—or for a month.

"You're the only person I know who talks about this stuff. Why don't you write a book for people like us?"

So I did.

This book is for all adults, because whether you are eventing at Preliminary, just learning how to post, or wondering whether you can add a new sport to your already busy lives, you have much more in common with one another than you do with children.

Riding is different for adults because life is different for adults. Our bodies have changed, we are concerned with different health and fitness issues, and our minds are more preoccupied with the facts of our professional lives.

My aim is to help you to understand yourself, your horse, and your sport, and to help you to avoid mistakes and disappointments. Everyone experiences some difficulties along the way, but many problems can be avoided entirely if you are able to anticipate them; and others can be overcome.

This applies to all riders at whatever level: beginner, intermediate, or advanced. I also try, wherever possible, to offer suggestions and alternatives that will suit those who have more money than time, more time than money, or a moderate amount of both.

What you get out of your association with horses will depend on what you put into it, and there are some things that you will need. Fortunately, these things are available to everyone regardless of income, ambitions, or amount of leisure time: manners, respect, and consideration for the animal.

Unless your interest is strictly limited to the mechanics of riding—and I hope it is not—you are about to become involved in a process of constant learning. You can never know it all. In fact, the more you know, the more you will find that there is left to learn, which is why the best riders and horsemen are also the most humble.

For you, as an adult rider, much of the fun of riding will be found in the process of improving your communication with your horse, and in the constant striving to refine your skills. Whether your dream involves Olympic dressage, endurance riding, or peaceful weekend trail rides through the woods, the process of learning can provide you with limitless challenge and infinite enjoyment.

This book does not go into detail about how to saddle a horse, clean a bridle, post or sit the trot. There are many wonderful how-to horse books already in print; some of them are listed in the Appendix. Instead, this book goes into some depth regarding the "what to," "why to," and even "when to." After many years of teaching both adults and children, I have found that children are invariably concerned with the "how" of things. Adults, although they too need to know *what* to do, are much more interested in the "why," and want deeper and more detailed explanations.

The underlying assumption of this book is that the readers, whether beginners or accomplished riders, are mature adults. They make their own decisions, pay their own bills, and budget their own time. Some may have money and time to spare, but most will be people who work from nine to five.

There are some things this book will do for you:

- Help you examine your reasons for riding and set realistic goals for yourself

- Offer suggestions and exercises that will allow you to achieve and maintain a level of fitness appropriate for riding

- Make you aware of the qualities to look for in stables, instructors, and horses; make you equally aware of characteristics to avoid, and of warning signs to be heeded

- Help you learn to use your lesson time to the best possible advantage

- Teach you how to find and care for the equipment you will need for yourself and your horse, and explain where it is safe to make compromises

- Introduce some basic concepts of riding, and address the issue of riding and training alone safely and efficiently

- Enable you to discuss your horse's health and communicate more effectively with your veterinarian

- Help you get the most from riding in shows and clinics, with emphasis on the benefits of preparation

- Explore the meaning of horsemanship, and examine the ways in which understanding the horse's physical and psychological nature will improve your riding and training

There is one final point:

You know more than you think you do, and you're better prepared than you think you are—you just haven't put it all together. You may think that you don't know enough to choose a good boarding barn, but you're not totally in the dark. Choosing a barn is a lot like choosing a daycare center. You want one that's clean and safe, where the other children are happy and where the staff is caring and professional. In both cases, you need to know specific things to look for, but a lot of the same standards apply.

Fitness is fitness. Riding fitness is not that different—you don't have to add extra time to your exercise program, just spend the same amount of time doing things that will help your riding.

Barns, instructors, lessons, horses—you know more about these things than you realize. A lot of the skills you already employ in other areas of your life can be applied to riding and horse ownership.

You need two things: information, and a way to integrate that information with all the things you already know. It is my hope that this book will provide you with both.

The Advantages of Maturity

There are several types of adult riders: beginning riders, returning riders, and continuing riders.

Beginning riders include those who did not ride as children and are just beginning to ride, and those who have just begun to think about learning to ride.

Returning riders are those who rode as children but have been away from the sport for many years. These riders must regain lost skills and learn new ones.

Continuing riders are those who have always ridden, and intend to ride forever, but whose bodies and situations have changed over the years.

Riding Realities

Adults who want to ride have to deal with several issues: managing the sport's demands on their time, their finances, and their bodies.

The adult body tends to be stiffer. It bends less easily, breaks more easily, and already has a certain amount of damage from injuries sustained over the years since childhood. And in most cases, it is less fit than it was during childhood.

Beginning riders, with no basis for comparison, are not concerned or distressed if they progress slowly or have a few aches and pains along the way. Continuing riders are usually reasonably fit, and have a realistic idea of what they can and cannot do.

Returning riders may have the most difficult time, as they are now struggling to do what they remember doing easily as children. Physical limitations, whether a low fitness level or an ailment such as arthritis, can impose unanticipated problems.

Other things have changed since they last rode. The popularity of different horse breeds, showing conditions, rules, and riding techniques are all different. Fashions in clothing and tack have changed, some drastically. Today's preferred headgear, for instance, is a tough protective helmet with a strong harness to keep it in place.

Riding requires more commitment now than it did fifteen, twenty, or thirty years ago; liability and litigation have imposed major changes. Many rental stables closed when insurance rates soared; riders must now find lesson stables or pay to board horses of their own. The cost of riding has increased dramatically; anyone who thinks in terms of the old prices for lessons, boarding, entry fees, and tack is in for a shock.

Nonetheless, adults are finding ways to ride. Whether they are beginning, returning, or have never left the sport, they have somehow managed to find, take, or create time for riding.

Special Considerations

Some physical and emotional aspects of adulthood make it more difficult to take up a new sport. Adults generally have increased weight, decreased physical strength, slower reflexes, and a sense of their own mortality.

Some of these factors can be changed; some we can come to terms with. Our weight and our strength are, to a great extent, under our control. Chapter 3 deals with determining, establishing, and maintaining a suitable fitness level.

Physical

Adult riders, especially beginners, should be aware of their physical limitations and their medical history. Ailments, illnesses, previous injuries, and bad backs may not be under our control in the sense that we can eliminate them, but they don't have to keep us from riding. We can learn to manage these conditions in the context of our sport. None of us can turn the clock back, but we can all eat and exercise for maximum health, and become more fit and strong. In the meantime, we can also be realistic. We can wrap our weak ankles, and wear back supports if we need them.

Adults must deal with riding and horse management issues that are affected by their own physical problems. An asthmatic person living where winters are severe, and who knows that she will be unable to ride during the coldest months, might plan to turn her horse out for the winter or lease him to someone else during those months. A rider with limited flexibility in her hands would find wide, thick reins easier to hold than narrow, thin ones, and would ride most comfortably in gloves year-round. A rider with hip problems would be happier riding a narrow horse and using a mounting block at all times. Any rider suffering from tension and stiffness, whether from lack of fitness or as a result of previous injury, can benefit immensely from slow stretching exercises.

Mental-Emotional

The challenge of riding is different for adults. This is true both for physical reasons and because the emotional involvement of adults is not the same as that of children. Learning to ride, or learning to ride better, are definite accomplishments, but adult egos are sometimes too involved.

Children are delighted just to have a chance to ride, but adults put a premium on the importance of doing it well and often feel that they "should" be good immediately. They often assume that if they can't be good at riding immediately, they will never be good at it.

Children are generally unconcerned about the possibility of failure—they are "going to learn to ride," not "going to try to learn to ride." When something goes wrong, the child rider usually reacts with annoyance or frustration, and blames something external: the horse, the saddle, or the jump. The adult rider, especially the adult beginner, reacts quite differently. Adults tend to anticipate failure and worry about its implications. And when something goes wrong, adults tend to assume the blame.

Adults must understand that (a) they are *not* the cause of everything that doesn't go perfectly, and (b) if they do cause a problem, they can take steps to correct the situation. But their tendency to assume the blame can also work *for* them: by assuming the responsibility, they retain the power to do something about the problem themselves.

A related difficulty is that often, for reasons of general fitness or specific injury or ailment, an adult who understands an instruction or an idea *perfectly* will not be able to put it into practice, or will have to struggle to achieve it. This often causes distress, frustration, and a feeling of "I'll never be able to do this; I'm too old, too stiff, too sore, too slow" on the part of the rider.

If you see riding as yet another arena in which to "prove" yourself, the result can be discouragement and depression. Instead of a source of relaxation and personal fulfillment, riding will then become just another source of stress. Don't let this happen. Adults must make use of their special advantages: maturity and a sense of perspective. Whatever the problem is, time, practice, patience, and a few compromises will usually solve it. Horses and riding can and should be a source of pleasure and personal fulfillment for you.

Adult Characteristics

A long attention span is one of the most useful assets a rider can possess—and most adults have it.

Adults can grasp the importance of learning the basic principles of equitation, and they understand why they must build a foundation by doing exercises, practicing basic skills, and learning the correct position.

Adults understand the principle of delayed gratification. They realize that the sooner the position and basic exercises become automatic, the sooner they can go on to the "fun stuff," riding the dressage test or the cross-country course.

Self-consciousness—in the sense of awareness, not embarrassment—is a characteristic of adult riders. This works both for and against them. They pay great attention to where their body parts are, which is good. They also make every effort to use deliberate control at all times, which is not always good: it can impair their ability to relax and go with the horse's movement.

Fear

Physical Fear

Most adult riders experience fear of one sort or another. Physical fear is simple and straightforward: the rider is afraid of falling and afraid of sustaining an injury. Adults, especially those new to riding, tend to be more fearful than child riders. This is reasonable, since adult bodies are older, stiffer, and often overweight. Adults have also been around longer than children, and in addition to the normal wear and tear on their bodies, they have had many more years in which to accumulate injuries, whether on the tennis court, on the ski slopes, or in the family car. Furthermore, adult injuries often have more wide-reaching implications than those of children. A bad fall for an adult is likely to be much more serious, both physically and financially, than it would be for an eleven-year-old.

Physical fear is not something that adults or their instructors should attempt to ignore, or deny. Physical fear is a reality. Riders can help themselves by entrusting their education to an understanding instructor, by taking safety precautions, and by being realistic about their physical capabilities. As their riding progresses, their increasing fitness, competence, confidence, and security will alleviate much of their fear.

Mental Fear

Many adult riders, especially beginners, experience mental fear. They are afraid of looking foolish, of not being able to learn the techniques of riding, of not being able to do it right. People who are competent and capable in their professional field can become so worried about not being "good at riding" that their tension and fear make their worst nightmare come true: they become incapable of learning anything. A good instructor with a reliable horse can do a great deal to eliminate this particular fear. Unless the rider is actually incapacitated by mental fear, the instructor should be able to reduce the level of worry and tension dramatically within a few lessons.

Emotional Fear

Emotional fear can also be incapacitating. Riders who suffer from "nerves," or who worry that the horse—or the instructor—doesn't like them, can be difficult to help. But occasionally a solution is surprisingly simple. Sometimes emotional fear is based on real, solvable problems that don't originate with the rider. If your horse is unsuitable and you are uncomfortable riding him—and as a result cannot relax—then you should use another horse for your lessons. If your instructor doesn't make you feel good about yourself and your effort, if she uses humiliation or derision or intimidation as teaching tools, then you should use another instructor for your lessons. You cannot be expected to learn if you are uncomfortable, intimidated, or frightened. Avoid placing yourself, even temporarily, in such a situation.

Emotional fear, however, usually comes from something far removed from the barn and the horses. Try not to bring personal or work-related problems to the barn: your riding time is special, and should be sacrosanct. You will find that concentrating on a lesson or on a riding session will usually cause you to forget everything else. Horses can be wonderful therapy.

If your fears persist, you can deal with them in other ways. Sports psychology offers a number of methods to overcome many forms of fear. Visualizing and positive imaging can help riders avoid emotional fear before it begins. Riders who cannot prevent their fears can be taught to use real-time methods to diminish the physical and mental effects of fear. Yoga and deep breathing can help a rider who needs to restore internal calm. More difficult, but probably more helpful in the long term, is the rider's ability to establish a sense of perspective: "I do this for fun" is a much better working concept than "I do this to punish myself" or "I don't know why I do this."

Much of the fear and anxiety experienced by adult riders is based on the fact that they don't feel well-informed about horses, or competent around them. As they gain experience, their anxiety lessens. Experience tells you what is likely to happen and how to deal with it; knowledge, familiarity, and competence make you aware of the animal's physiology, psychology, and most likely moves and countermoves. Fear is a perfectly reasonable reaction in a person who knows that she doesn't know these things.

The Balancing Act: Riding versus Obligations

Only you can determine exactly how much time you will have for riding once you have met the obligations of job, home, and family, and only you know whether your finances can stretch to cover the needs of your sport. Stress levels and time factors vary widely. If you have a low-stress job, you may be able to put it behind you as you leave the office—or it may take you several hours of conscious effort to calm down after a day at a high-stress job.

Work that includes physical exercise can lower your stress level, and puts you at an advantage in terms of physical fitness. But too many of us spend our workdays sitting at a desk or a conference table. If you leave your job at 5:00 every weekday, take no work home with you, and own your weekends, your riding plan and exercise program can be very different from those of someone whose job demands take-home work, weekend meetings, and frequent travel.

Pregnancy

Pregnancy brings with it a number of physiological and psychological changes. Consult your doctor about riding during pregnancy. Many riders find that pregnancy presents no problem for the first few months, unless morning sickness interferes with their rides. Some doctors discourage women from riding during the first trimester because of the risk of miscarriage, and because light-headedness and fainting could result in serious falls. Many women can ride through mid-pregnancy with their doctors' permission, as long as they stay fit, take all proper precautions, and refrain from jumping and cross-country galloping. If you do choose to ride while pregnant, you will be pleased to know that maternity riding pants are now available. As for how soon to resume riding after giving birth, this depends on many different factors, so the most responsible advice to offer is "consult your doctor."

Drawing on my own experience as an instructor, I can say that the women who scheduled lessons six weeks after the baby's birth almost invariably rang up and canceled them a few days beforehand. They had overestimated the rate at which they would regain their strength, they had underestimated their pain and fatigue, and they had underestimated the level and depth of their fascination with the new little person in their lives. All of them resumed riding eventually—some when their babies were sleeping through the night, and some when their babies became toddlers.

Toddlers and Preschoolers

Horses are large, timid, excitable animals, and accidents happen very quickly around them; stables are not safe places for unattended children. It is all too easy for children to get into trouble or cause trouble for others without meaning to; it is also easy for them to get hurt. Leave your toddlers and preschoolers at home, unless you have brought them to the barn for a visit, to show them around and introduce them to your horse. If you are coming out to ride, leave the little ones at home—for their safety, for the safety of others, for your peace of mind, and for the sanity of the stable staff.

Although owners and managers will often bite their lips and say nothing in order not to offend paying boarders, child-care is not a service you can expect unless it is specifically mentioned in your boarding contract. No boarding stable—no stable of any kind, for that matter—was ever intended to function as a babysitting or child-minding service. If your stable actually offers a crèche or romper room as part of the facilities, then your stable is unique and you are unbelievably lucky.

School-Age Children

School-age children are another matter. If they are under your supervision, if they are taking lessons, or if they are doing barn chores by prior arrangement, then they have legitimate business at the stable. As long as they are quiet, well-behaved, and experienced in the ways of horses and stable etiquette, they should be welcome there. The same holds true for middle school and high school students, some of whom are wonderful horsemen, great company, and an asset to any stable.

If one of your reasons for riding is to promote a sport in which your whole family can be involved, then you probably bring both spouse and children to the barn on a regular basis. They may even take lessons or have horses of their own. Many families hunt together, show together, or come together to support the efforts of the family horseperson, whether that is Mom, Dad, or one of the children. If this describes your family, then by all means take your children to the stable. They are a part of the enterprise, they know what to do and how to behave, and they belong there.

Other People's Children

The reasons for leaving very small or undisciplined children at home will become perfectly clear to you the very first time someone else at your boarding stable doesn't do it. After just one evening of riding in an arena inhabited by screaming, running, climbing, blatantly-disregarding-all-standards-of-behavior-and-rules-of-safety children, you will feel exceedingly virtuous for leaving your own offspring at home, where they cannot endanger themselves, embarrass you, or be exposed to children like these.

Children are wonderfully creative, and can think of any number of activities that aren't covered by rules. They are also very literal. You may warn a child, "Don't run up behind the horse and grab his tail," or "Be sure to let the horse know you're there; don't come up to him without speaking to him first, and put a hand on him so that he'll know where you are." But behavior is a matter of degree, and will you think to say, "Oh, and don't run up behind the horse, yell at him, and whack him on the rump"?

You may tell a child, "You can't ride Beauty until she has finished her dinner," but will it occur to you that sitting on the horse isn't the same as "riding" and that you should have added, "While Beauty is eating, don't try to sit on her, and especially not by taking a chair into her stall and trying to climb onto her from the back of the chair"? Or—poor Beauty—will you notice if the child goes into her stall, takes the hay, and gives it to another horse so that Beauty will finish faster? And what if the next-door horse, who was delighted to get Beauty's hay, isn't supposed to be given alfalfa because of allergies?

Children can put horses at great risk, and they can put themselves at risk as well. The saintly old mare that allows children to crawl between her legs and under her belly does exist, but even she may kick at a fly without stopping to notice that Mark and Susie are in the way. Children at barns require supervision, full stop.

Children, no matter how well-behaved, can also distract you from your own riding. Even the most doting parent should ride and take her lessons in an atmosphere that allows her to concentrate on what she is doing. Even if your children are charming, tactful, expert equestrians and models of deportment, they will still be a distraction for you. Their presence puts you into parent mode—part of your mind will always be on them. And although this is absolutely appropriate for you as a parent, it is inappropriate for you as a rider because it limits the concentration you can bring to your riding, your horse, and your instructor.

Riding with Children

Sharing an arena, or a group lesson, with children can make you feel awkward, especially if you are the only adult in the group, or if you are the least proficient rider. It can be frustrating to be surrounded by little riders who are much further along than you are. It will take time for you to change your skill level, and it's not always easy to change your feelings. But you *can* give yourself a different perspective.

The task you have taken on is to become as good a rider as you possibly can without wasting your time and emotions on pointless comparisons. Don't allow yourself to feel frustrated, or awed, just because there are children who ride better than you do. They are probably not prodigies, but they *are* more experienced: they've been at this longer than you have. The annoying twelve-year-old in your group may have started riding at age eight and so—if you insist on looking at it that way—is four years "ahead" of you. So what?

If you truly dislike being surrounded by children, you do have options. You can keep your horse at a stable that caters primarily to adults, or you can ride at hours that are less appealing to (or impossible for) children who are in school.

If you are competition-oriented and prefer to spend your time with adults, you might consider focusing on dressage since there are so many adults competing.

Adults as Role Models

Children will look up to you just because you *are* an adult. Even if you lack experience with horses, children will assume that you possess maturity and judgment. You may be a novice, but you are still a role model. So wear your helmet, wear your boots, observe safety precautions, and treat your horse well. Do it for your own safety, do it because it's right, and do it because you have an influence on younger riders.

Children are quick to notice the difference between what adults say and what they do. It does no good to talk to children about safety or to explain precisely why it is dangerous to ride without helmets, if we ride without helmets ourselves. The messages we are sending to the children are these: first, that helmets are just for kids, a sort of badge of immaturity; and second, that the "mature" person is somehow immune to head injuries. Children see everything, and are very likely to do what they see adults do, even if the adults are acting foolishly.

Adult Advantages

The advantages of adulthood far outweigh the disadvantages. Mature riders are comfortable dealing with concepts, ideas, and pattern recognition. Riding, for them, is a more complex, more intellectual pursuit.

Adult beginners still have to learn the basics of the sport—there is no way around the need to acquire proper technique—but many adults value communication over control, finesse over force. The young may come to this in time, if they stay with the sport and if they are focused and driven and feel a need to improve. For an adult, this can be the starting point.

Adults have a mature perspective, the ability to focus, and the habit of learning. They are more aware of their motivations and goals; their ambitions are more directed.

Adults can make a realistic commitment to their sport, taking into account their time and money limitations, and the limitations imposed by their physical condition, ailments, fitness level, and professional and social obligations.

Adults make good students. They know how to learn and how to extract the most important concepts from a lesson. Adults can also evaluate and assimilate information in a way that a child cannot.

Adults are organized planners, and are generally good at setting realistic long-term, intermediate, and short-term goals. Through experience, most adults have learned patience. The concept of delayed gratification is more real to adults than it is to children, who have a limited time-frame and who want it all and want it now.

Adults have more physical awareness. They are better able to understand the stresses on their bodies, and the results of those stresses. And they know that they must consider the long-term implications of stress and injury, in terms of their family life and of their employment.

Adults have empathy. Most adults work or have worked, and are able to understand the horse as a creature with a job to do. Adults know the advantages of having a good boss. They can understand that their horse works for a living and that his job is to respond as best he can—based on his understanding, abilities, and training—to the demands of his rider.

Adults know about job satisfaction. They understand that the job conditions are as important as—and often more important than—the work itself. If you feel competent to do your work, if you are allowed to do it in a physically and emotionally comfortable atmosphere, if you receive respect and appreciation and rewards for your success, then you will be happy in your job. If the atmosphere is uncomfortable and you get no respect, appreciation, or even consideration, you will be unhappy even if the work itself is interesting and worth doing.

Your horse doesn't intellectualize this, but his situation is similar. The key difference is that *all* of your horse's job satisfaction comes from feeling comfortable, competent, and appreciated. Most working adults have had a few "bad boss" experiences, and have felt that they would do things differently if they were in charge. Your horse will give you a chance to do just that. Treat him as you would want to be treated by your employer—fairly, kindly, and with respect.

Riding is a wonderful sport because it goes beyond the merely physical. Your horse will benefit from the years you have spent learning to develop and appreciate the best human qualities, such as kindness and compassion, understanding, tolerance, patience, and goodwill. You will appreciate your horse's generosity and his willingness to give you the benefit of the doubt. Whatever your experience and ambitions, riding can bring you immense physical and psychological benefits. This book will help you maximize those benefits: if you are aware and prepared, you will encounter fewer problems and have more fun.

Reasons for Riding

You want to ride, but what exactly does that mean? Who are you, what is your life like, what are the constraints on your time, why do you want to ride, and what sort of riding do you want to do? If you are just beginning in this sport, why did you choose riding? If you have been riding all your life, why do you continue to ride? And if you rode at one time and are now taking up riding again, why are you returning to the sport?

The better you understand yourself, your life, your reasons for wanting to ride, and the time and money that you can afford to invest in riding, the better your choices and decisions will be. This chapter will help you look more closely at your motivations, your ambitions, your level of fitness, and your professional, social, and financial realities.

Some people are attracted to the challenge of learning to ride. Others look forward to the challenge of competition. For many people, riding represents the fulfillment of a lifetime dream; their finances or life situations have finally allowed them to begin. Some riders enjoy riding because it gets them away from their families for a while; others enjoy riding because it allows them to involve their families.

Everyone has different ambitions and expectations, but all riders and potential riders should think seriously about the amount of time, energy, and money they can afford to invest in their riding.

Beth Saupe, 41, married, two children at home, vet technician in the surgical department of the small animal clinic at the University of Illinois, and "Topper" (Angel's Top Trophy, Morgan gelding):

"My long-term goal is to see how far my horse and I can go in eventing. My immediate goals are to improve my own position and to concentrate on getting pure gaits and good transitions.

"Right now I'm very focused on dressage. I started taking dressage lessons to improve my eventing, but I've begun to enjoy it for its own sake; I'm beginning to feel the finesse and subtlety of it. And it's made a big difference to my jumping— I have more input, it's more of a partnership now, not just the horse saying 'Let's GO!' and me either saying 'Okay' and being carried along or saying 'NO' and having a fight. I enjoy competitions more now."

Know Your Physical Self

Evaluate your physical attributes. There is more to this than simply writing down your height, weight, and basic build, although this information is important. For riding, you will need to consider other factors because they will determine the sort of exercise plan you will need to achieve your desired level of riding fitness. They will also, to some extent, dictate the sort of tack and saddlery you will need, the sort of horse you will find most comfortable, and even the type of riding that will suit you best.

Analyze your physique. Do you have a short torso and long legs, or vice versa? Are your muscles typically loose or tight? Would you describe yourself as supple or stiff? Do you think of yourself as coordinated or uncoordinated? What previous sports have you enjoyed? When you participated in those sports, were you competitive, or did you play just for fun? The skills you used for ice skating, diving, or tennis can all be helpful to your riding.

All riders have to take their fitness level into consideration. If your schedule won't permit daily riding, you will have to consider how long it takes you to become fit—and how quickly you can become unfit. And you will need to budget time for fitness. Are you a high-energy person or a low-energy person? What are your sleep requirements and your sleep patterns? It may be that on paper you could ride every day by getting up two hours earlier each morning—but in reality would this work? Or do those hours provide you with desperately needed sleep?

Where Does Riding Fit into Your Life?

There are other questions you should ask yourself. Once you have looked beyond the fundamental idea of riding, what exactly do you want to *do* with a horse? And will your schedule and your energy allow you to do it? Exactly what sort of a horse do you have, or do you want? Something that can come out of a stall three times a week and remain calm and quiet while you ride gently for half an hour? Or are you thinking of something that you can ride twice a day for an hour or two and take to competitions on weekends?

Motivations

There are many different reasons for riding. Some of the ones I've listed here may help you to examine your own motivations.

Mastery   Some people enjoy riding because it gives them a feeling of power over a large animal.

Showing   Some people prefer the competitive aspect of riding.

Family Togetherness   Riding can bring family members together in a common endeavor, with everyone participating.

Personal Focus   Riding can be a wonderful way to escape from your family and do something that is just for yourself.

Health and Exercise   Riding can be an enjoyable form of exercise, and an effective one—especially if you also groom and muck out.

Therapy   Riding can be wonderful therapy for the physically disabled and the mentally handicapped, but anyone can benefit from the therapeutic aspects of horses and riding. Riding can help adults release their tension after a long and stressful workday.

Horse as Companion   For many people, the companionship of a horse is an important part of their daily life. A good relationship with a horse takes time and care and considerate, consistent handling; when you have achieved this, it becomes one of the most significant relationships in your life.

Styles and Forms of Riding

Pleasure Riding, Trail Riding, and Hacking   People who ride for recreation often prefer trail riding. It provides them with a peaceful way to relax and enjoy nature, scenery, and wildlife.

Eventing   Many riders view eventing as the ultimate horse sport, combining as it does the precision of dressage, the speed and excitement of cross-country jumping, and the accuracy of show jumping.

Dressage   Many riders turn to dressage because they appreciate the precision and control it requires. Others may enjoy the process of developing subtle communication with their horses, and the challenge of bringing out the horses' potential as well as their own. Dressage riders can continue to ride into their later years, which is not always an option for eventers.

Competitive Trail Riding   Trail riding can be much, much more than a relaxing ramble through the woods. Competitive trail riding can be challenging and exciting, and it requires that horse and rider undergo serious physical preparation.

Long-Distance Riding, Endurance Riding   These are similar to competitive trail riding but require an even higher level of horse and rider fitness and conditioning.

Your Expectations

Whatever your riding preference, you will be happier if you begin with realistic expectations, based on your own and your horse's physical abilities and fitness. You will also need to be realistic about the amount of time and money you can put into your sport, and about the degree of commitment you can make to it. It is largely true that with riding, as with almost anything else, you will get out of it what you put into it. What are you looking for? What do you want? How much do you want it? What are you willing to do to get it? Evaluating your reasons for riding may help you to understand what riding means to you, and whether it is a pastime, a hobby, a sport, an obsession, or something else altogether.

Goal Setting

Before you begin to define and set your goals, think about what you want from your riding. Whether riding is new to you or whether you spent your entire childhood on horseback, you will need to consider your ambitions and desires as they apply to riding. What are your larger, long-term goals? Not your dreams—although most of us enjoy the occasional Olympic medal fantasy—but your actual, practical, real-time goals? What do you want? Do you want competitive success? Is your goal the acquisition of a new physical skill? Or do you want to improve and refine your communication with horses?

Dreams

You will need to distinguish between your goals and your dreams. Dreams are wonderful, but they are not goals: they make no demands on us, they don't challenge us, we don't actually have to *do* anything about them. Dreams are pleasant fantasies, not actual ambitions. Don't lose your dreams—a good winning-the-gold-medal fantasy is a lovely counterpoint to tack-cleaning or braiding. But keep your dreams in their place. Don't let them take over your riding life, or you may find yourself wandering around the arena on a loose rein, daydreaming, instead of working towards a realistic goal that could provide you with real satisfaction.

Goals

Your goals can be divided into long-term goals, intermediate goals, and short-term goals. Your long-term goals are your major objectives; your intermediate goals are the milestones on the way to those objectives, and your short-term goals are the daily markers that you will use in your everyday work. For example, if your long-term goal is to jump a 3' course at a hunter show, your intermediate goals might be competing successfully over courses set at 2'6" and 2'9" and schooling over a 3' course at home. Your short-term goals might be learning to count strides, learning to change leads, and learning to ride a bending line. If you break your short-term goals down into smaller, simpler elements, you might find yourself practicing simple lead changes on straight lines, or counting strides out loud on your way around the arena to a pole on the ground.

Setting goals for yourself is a useful way of tracking your progress. This can help you keep an accurate perspective on your achievements. In September, when you are frustrated with your inability to maintain your horse's bend on a 15-meter circle, it will help your emotional state immensely if you can look back through your notes and see that you have indeed been making progress. In fact, it may even provide you with an ego boost if you discover that in April your goal for September had been to ride your horse forward on straight lines and begin work on 20-meter circles. Similarly, if you are unhappy with a horse that leaps every tiny stream on the trail in October, it will make you feel much better to remember that in June he was too nervous to go out alone and wouldn't cross water even in company.

Manage Your Goals

For your own sake, set realistic, attainable goals. If you set unreasonable or impractical goals for yourself—riding every day for two hours, say, when your schedule allows you to get to the barn only four days each week—you will feel frustration and guilt instead of pleasure and satisfaction. If you are in doubt about what is possible for you, remember that goals—as opposed to dreams—should be attainable, and you should be able to reconcile them with the rest of your life. Don't set yourself up for failure. If you are able to ride for one hour three times a week, the Olympics may be your dream but ought not to be your goal.

If every other rider at your boarding barn seems to be seventeen, physically fit, rich, and an "A" circuit competitor, don't let yourself imagine that you are somehow inferior. If your realistic personal goal is success on the circuit, then learn from the other riders' example. If you enjoy trail riding on your dependable, friendly horse and have no competitive ambitions whatsoever, don't feel that you need to apologize for anything. Competition is only one aspect of riding, and not everyone is driven to compete.

Don't set your goals too high, but don't set them too low either. You shouldn't sell yourself short. Learn to know yourself: your abilities, your resources, your ambitions. All too often, people imagine that they don't want anything, not because they are truly contented but because they won't allow themselves to want something they think they can't have. Learning how to want something—or admitting to yourself that you want something—can be much harder than the physical process of learning to ride.

When you know what you want, figure out whether it is possible. If it is, plan a way to attain it. Any restrictions you place on yourself should be based on physical reality: your expectations shouldn't exceed your capabilities or those of your horse. You can reset your goals at any time, so it makes sense to begin by setting goals that are challenging but definitely achievable. It will be much easier on your ego if you need to revise your goals upwards than if you set them too high and have to revise them downwards. Set yourself up for success, and remember that you are always free to change your goals to match changes in your lifestyle or your interests. And always remember that a goal without a plan is just a dream.

It's Never Too Late

If you have begun riding as an adult, you aren't doomed to be a permanent beginner. If you lack the resources or the ambition to be highly competitive, this doesn't mean that you have to limit yourself to one aspect of your chosen sport. The horse sports you enjoy watching on television and reading about in magazines—showing, jumping, dressage, driving, and so on—can all be pursued and enjoyed at a lesser level. If your ambitions are modest, you can still have competitive goals. Many competitions are perfectly accessible to the ordinary or weekend rider with an ordinary, solid-citizen horse. Your options are open. You can prepare, you can compete, you can place, and you can win. Even if you were a successful competitor as a child, you may find that the success you achieve later in life means more to you than those earlier ribbons did. Now that you have to work harder for your ribbons, you may appreciate them more.

Basic Goals   A riding student's goals should include the desire to acquire a thorough knowledge of horsemanship, the desire to acquire a compassionate manner towards horses, and an honest desire to ride correctly.

Personal Goals   Personal goals have to do with character development. These might include becoming more patient, becoming more understanding, or even—very specifically—learning to put your horse away and go for a walk instead of having a fight with the animal.

Riding Goals   Riding goals are related to very specific skills. Examples of riding goals might be learning to sit the trot, learning to ask for (and get) a flying change or an extended trot, learning to open and close a gate from horseback, and learning to jump ditches and banks.

Competitive Goals   If your heart is set on participating in—or winning—a particular competition, make that your long-term goal. Then analyze the skills you will need to participate or to win, and make those skills your intermediate goals. Take each specific skill, break it down into smaller units, and you will make each of these pieces a short-term goal.

Some goals, like dressage tests, are already broken up into pieces for you: each movement can and should be learned separately before you put them all together for a specific test. Other goals, like a specific horse trial or event, break logically into their three phases: dressage, cross-country, and stadium. Each phase can be further broken down for your convenience. For stadium, specific goals might include learning to shorten and lengthen your horse's stride at the canter, learning to ride turns and bending lines accurately, and learning to go forward towards unfamiliar jumps. For cross-country, specific goals might include learning to jump ditches, banks, drops, and water; learning how to estimate your speed; learning how to keep your horse balanced over rolling or hilly terrain.

These are only a few suggestions; there are thousands of possibilities. The important thing to remember is that any general goal, such as "riding Third Level Test Two" or "riding in a Training-Level event," should be broken down into smaller, specific, manageable pieces. Keeping your short-term and intermediate goals in mind will help you keep your perspective. This will help you with specific incidents and problems. Your response to your horse shying at the judge's stand, for instance, won't be "Oh, we'll *never* get to Second Level," which is an understandable but unhelpful reaction. If you keep your goals in mind, you will be able to react in a more constructive way. Your response might be, "We need a *round* circle here, and this horse needs to be paying attention to *me*," or "OK, next time I'll ask for more forward movement and more bend *before* we get close to the stand, and we'll just cruise right by it."

A regular review of your goals and your success in meeting them will also help when you want to assess your progress and revise your general plan. If you can look through a list of your short-term goals from three months ago, you will be able to see which goals still need to be met (Champion isn't really flexing his hocks yet, and he isn't moving forward enough into his downward transitions). But you will also be able to recognize those goals you *have* met (Champion stays quietly on the bit at all three gaits, and almost all his halts are square now) and feel justifiably pleased with yourself and your horse as a result.

Dealing with Failure

No matter what your long-term goals may be, there is one goal that all riders should include in their list: learning to deal with failure. If you believe that the only success is formal recognition—the ribbon or the trophy—then you will feel like a failure when you don't get those rewards. Setting specific short-term goals can help you adjust your thinking.

A Case History

In March, 37-year-old Sarah decided that her end-of-season goal would be to compete successfully at a Training Level event. Her horse was quiet and obedient in the dressage arena, but he was afraid of ditches and water. He was difficult to steer at the gallop, and he was not very fit. In September, after six months of conditioning and three wins at Novice, Sarah competed at Training Level, did her best, and placed out of the ribbons. Sarah had failed—or had she?

Sarah was disappointed, but she sat down and reviewed her rides. Her horse had been tense in the dressage arena and had bucked twice, hurting his score. Sarah thought about this and realized that she had worked so hard to improve his cross-country performance that she had not really paid much attention to his dressage, which had always been good enough to win at Novice. Her horse was fitter now, and needed a longer warm-up and a more focused rider. This was something she could work on.

Sarah's hard work had paid off on the cross-country course. Her horse was so fit that he wasn't even breathing hard when he finished. Steering had been no problem, even at a gallop. He had trotted through the water without hesitating, and he had taken the ditch in stride. But he had stopped twice: at the Helsinki and at the drop fence. Sarah thought about this and realized that she had not really planned how or where to jump the Helsinki; she had just ridden her horse towards the unfamiliar fence and assumed that he would jump. Just when Sarah should have been telling him "We're going to jump this," she had left him on his own, and he had stopped. The problem at the drop fence had been hers, too: Sarah had never jumped such a large drop, and she had been intimidated. She had ridden more and more slowly on the approach, and by the time they reached it, her horse had received her message loud and clear: "This is a scary fence, let's not go."

Sarah learned three things from her experience. First, she understood that if she analyzed what she was doing and didn't like it, she could change it. Second, she learned that her system of setting small, manageable goals was a good system: A year ago, her horse would have stopped at the water and the ditch, and he would have been exhausted by the time he passed between the finish flags. Third, Sarah learned that her plan must be flexible—and would need to change as her horse changed. She could create a more lengthy and demanding dressage warmup as her horse became more fit; she was free to reassess her situation and change her goals whenever a change was called for. But overall, Sarah was not unhappy with her experience. She could see her progress, and felt that her ride had been a success even though she had come home without a ribbon.

As an adult, Sarah had a great advantage when it came to setting, meeting, and changing her goals. She took responsibility for her horse's preparation and performance, and was realistic about the changes she had made and those she still needed to make.

Setting Yourself Up to Succeed

Adults have tremendous advantages when it comes to goal-setting: maturity and realism. Children too often confuse dreams with goals; they just want to *be* the latest Olympic or World Champion, whereas adults have an idea of the time, effort, and expense such an achievement requires. As an adult, you can be limited by your realism, or you can set yourself up to succeed.

You should begin by setting modest, attainable goals for yourself. That way, you can have success after success, and you can revise your goals later as you become more confident. It is a much better strategy than setting unrealistic goals that you cannot possibly achieve—saying to yourself "I want to win everything and be the best rider in the world"—and then failing time after time. You will probably fail at some point—we all do. Allow yourself to accept it, pick yourself up, and move on. You can't possibly improve your skills if you don't make a commitment, put something on the line, and take the risk that you might fail. It isn't permanent, and it can teach you something that will help you succeed the next time.

Your Instructor and Your Goals

If you have an instructor, enlist her assistance with your goal-setting. Her experience and knowledge will help you set realistic, attainable goals for yourself. She will also be able to incorporate your goals—long-term, intermediate, and short-term—into your lesson program. Let your instructor know if your goals change and if your health, your finances, or your interests are responsible for the change.

Working towards Your Goals

How good a rider do you want to be, and how much effort are you willing to put into becoming a good rider? Riding is a strange sport. It is not unusual to find someone who "wants to be a really good rider" but who would never even think of devoting the same time and effort to riding that she would consider to be necessary if she wanted to become a really good dancer, swimmer, or figure-skater.

Making Your Work Count

Time counts, mileage counts, quality time counts. Many riders consider themselves lucky if they can ride for an hour or so, three times a week. If you are one of these riders, take heart—those three days can benefit both horse and rider immensely *if* they are prepared and they work hard.

If your horse can be turned out, he will be more likely to settle into his work without requiring an initial period of freedom to blow off steam. This can save you time at the beginning of each ride, and it will also give you a fitter horse with which to work.

Maintaining your own fitness can save time as well. If you are fit, the physical stress of your time in the saddle will be minimized. If you rode as a youngster and are just returning to the sport, you are probably less fit now, so don't expect to pick up precisely where you remember leaving off. In chapter 3, you will learn ways to achieve and maintain riding fitness.

Two or three hours of trail riding, although enjoyable, will *not* develop the horse's "ring of muscles" even if you do it daily. But forty-five minutes of concentrated *work*, even three times a week, will produce visible results for both rider and horse. Then, when you go out on the trails, those rides will give you a lovely change of pace and a chance to relax and enjoy the scenery.

Help Yourself

Make an honest examination of your reasons for riding, and then spend some time considering your goals. This will be one of the best time-investments you could possibly make. Think about what you can bring to your sport; think about what you want to get out of it. If your motivations and your goals are compatible, and can be reconciled with the physical and financial realities of your life, you will be as prepared and in control as anyone could be.

Regardless of your experience, your abilities, and your resources, you will benefit from analyzing your motives and setting goals for yourself. This self-analysis is available to every rider; it isn't just for people who want to ride in competitions. Whatever your riding interests, provide yourself with goals and a plan to achieve them. Goals and plans allow you to track your progress; preparation and planning will save you time and effort by allowing you to direct your energy in a systematic, constructive way. The reward is built-in: your riding will become more enjoyable as you set and meet your goals.

Rider Fitness

"Riding isn't really exercise—the horse does all the work!" You've probably heard this before; unfortunately, it simply isn't true.

One of the most appealing aspects of riding is that it can be done, in some form, by almost anyone regardless of age or ability. But whether your riding involves daily schooling for competition, a weekly lesson, or just enjoying the companionship of a horse on occasional trail rides, it is impossible to overestimate the importance of physical fitness.

Fitness increases our ability to meet the physical demands of riding. It enhances our enjoyment, lessens our risk, and allows us to make the most of our riding time. Adults—especially busy, working adults, and what other kind is there?—are often not very fit. Sometimes they are very unfit indeed. If you have never considered fitness a goal, riding may cause you to reconsider. Horses can't perform well unless they are fit; the same is true of riders. Your fitness will help your progress and your horse's performance. It will also make you a safer rider.

Fitness is one of the best possible forms of rider protection. Your joints, muscles, and tendons all act as shock absorbers. If they are fit, conditioned, and warm, you will be flexible and supple. A flexible and supple person is less likely to incur riding injuries. A fit body can move more quickly, react more accurately and with less effort, avoid or prevent accidents, and retain control of the horse and the situation more effectively than can an unfit body.

Fitness makes us more effective riders.

Types of Fitness

Good riding requires that the rider possess concentration, balance, re-laxation, and the ability to apply a variety of aids singly and together. In physical terms, this means that you must have endurance, strength, and the ability to coordinate many muscle groups. Riding requires several forms of fitness.

Endurance   Aerobic fitness enables a rider to maintain position and balance over time without having to stop and rest.

Strength   Resistance training builds muscle mass and power by increas-ing the ability of muscles to contract.

Flexibility   Joint motion, muscle stretching, general suppleness.

The combination of endurance, strength, and flexibility will increase your coordination. Riders need to be able to use many muscles and muscle groups, singly and in combination, for smooth and efficient acting and reacting: following the horse's moves, countering the horse's moves, and staying on when a move is extreme or unexpected.

Riders *can* get and stay fit if their only exercise is riding—but it isn't easy. Someone who rides five or six horses each day may not require any other form of exercise. Someone who rides actively every other day and pursues another form of exercise can stay fit enough to ride, as long as the riding itself is not too demanding. For most working riders, such schedules are unrealistic. You may ride only three days a week—and there may be times when you can't ride at all, because of the weather or because of the seasonal demands of your work. Irregular and weekend riders cannot depend on their riding for even a moderate amount of fitness. A well-planned exercise program will help you keep your riding muscles in shape.

Riding muscles are not just those used for mounting, dismounting, walk, trot, and canter, but also those involved in your reaction to the horse's unanticipated movements. A sudden shy or impromptu gallop depart will demand real physical strength on the part of the rider. If you are unfit, one active ride (imagine yourself on a recently clipped horse on a cold windy day) can sideline you for a week or longer. You can alleviate some of the pain and begin to repair the damage by helping your muscles relax and stretch, but no amount of liniment, Epsom salts, or massage will make up for a lack of physical preparation.

Achieving Fitness

Riding fitness can be achieved in two ways. Riders can either concentrate exclusively on exercises to prepare them for riding, or they can increase their overall fitness so that it carries over into their riding.

Resistance Training

Riders don't need bulky muscle—they need strength. The most direct way to increase muscle strength is through resistance training, also known as weight-lifting. Women can benefit tremendously from resistance training, and they will *not* bulk up like Mr. Olympia unless they work out six hours a day and take massive doses of steroids. As your muscles become stronger, you will feel less fatigue and fewer back pains, which will improve your riding. But don't rush into a weight-lifting program.

Riding muscles enable us to stay on the
horse at walk, trot, canter, and over jumps . . .

Check with your doctor first, and then start carefully and slowly. Save
time by taking your time.

If you belong to a health club that offers individual help from quali-
fied instructors, or if your club offers affordable classes, this is a good
way to commit to an exercise program. If your schedule won't allow you
to take classes, health clubs offer equipment and have someone on duty
who can demonstrate the various machines. If you don't have access to
a health club, perhaps you can find room for some exercise equipment
in your home. "Used" exercise benches and dumbbells are easy to
find, and generally inexpensive. Check the classified ads in your local
paper, or visit a store that recycles sports equipment. Most "used"
exercise equipment is barely used; in fact, some of it is unused, which is
probably why it is being resold.

Even if all the time you have for resistance training is twenty minutes three days a week, resistance training will improve your riding. You
will have increased muscle mass and stronger bones, as well as improved
balance, coordination, and flexibility, and better posture on and off the
horse.

. . . and must be strong and supple to cope with sudden, unexpected movements.

A rider's exercise program should include:

- Aerobic exercise for stamina: walking, jogging, swimming, skiing, bicycling

- Resistance training for strength: working out with weights to develop shoulders and arms, upper and lower back, thighs (especially adductors) and calves

- Stretching for overall flexibility and circulation

- Specific exercises to target body parts that are particularly important to riding, and that are especially subject to strain and injury

Self-Awareness

Many rider problems of position, technique, or effectiveness exist because one part of the body has been underdeveloped or developed incorrectly at the expense of another. We sometimes become impatient with our horses for being "one-sided": they tend to be more flexible in one direction than in the other. But we, too, are "one-sided" and unevenly developed. Be aware of your own one-sidedness. Would you like to understand your horse's problem better? Try to catch a ball, eat spaghetti, or brush your teeth with the hand you don't normally use. You'll have to make a deliberate effort; you will feel awkward, uncomfortable, "unnatural"; you may even drop the ball, the fork, or the toothbrush. One-sidedness promotes unevenness in humans, just as it does in horses. If you invariably sit with one leg crossed over the other, or read with your head tilted to one side, you are promoting unevenness. This will carry over into your riding. The cure is exercise designed to develop muscles correctly and in balance with other muscles. Your riding will benefit if you make good balance and good posture part of your daily life.

Essential Concepts in Fitness

Warming Up

Warming up and cooling down are essential processes for the horse *and* for the rider. Warming up is a literal term: the body warms up. The goal of a warmup is warmth and flexibility; sweating is not a problem, but you should not get out of breath.

Cooling Down

Cooling down, unlike warming up, is *not* a literal term. "Warming down" would be a much better description of the process. In any case, the point is to avoid losing heat too rapidly. Cooling down too quickly can lead to cramped muscles. Gentle, slow, continuous exercise, followed by stretching, is a useful way to cool down. For the horse, this might mean trotting gently for ten minutes or so after more active exercise, then walking for another ten minutes or longer, until the (slow) cooling-down process is complete. For the rider, the cooling-down process might be as simple as putting on a sweatshirt or a long-sleeved shirt while cooling down the horse. By the time the horse is cooled down, the rider will be, too. When exercising off the horse, use common sense: if you finish a strenuous workout abruptly and then stand in front of an air conditioner, you will be stiff and sore the next day.

Stretching

Stretching exercises are essential but are often left out of a rider's fitness program. Riders need stretched muscles, but riding does almost nothing to stretch them. Some stretching exercises can be done on the horse, preferably on the longe, but most should be done *off* the horse.

Daily stretching off the horse will benefit you in several ways: psychological, physical, and financial. First, you will get used to doing the exercises every day, wherever you are. Second, you will control the setting and the circumstances in which you exercise; there will be no chance that a sudden movement from a startled horse could cause you to tear a muscle you were trying to stretch. And third, by doing your warmup and stretching on a regular basis and especially just before your riding lesson, you will be able to use more of your lesson time for the lesson itself.

Always warm up first, then stretch, not the other way around. Warming up relaxes your muscles and allows them to stretch; warm, stretched muscles are much less likely to be injured by sudden movements. The order of work for you and your horse should always be: warmup, stretch, strengthen, stretch, cool down.

General Guidelines for Stretching:

1. *Stretch slowly*, hold the position, but *do not bounce*. Think yoga, not aerobics. Bouncing can be dangerous, and it's counterproductive: it tightens the very muscles that you are trying to stretch.

2. *Stretch gently*, and never to the point of pain. Take your time, listen to your body, and stop before you feel pain.

3. *Stretch at your own rate*. As your muscles learn to stretch and contract effectively, you will become more flexible. Don't look at other people and assume that you should stretch as easily and as well as they do. They have different bodies, different fitness histories, and different genetics—some people are naturally more flexible than others.

4. *Stretch thoroughly;* allow yourself twenty minutes per session. If you are travelling, attending a conference, sitting for hours, and accumulating a lot of tension, begin and end each day by going for a walk and then stretching for twenty minutes.

You will be glad you invested the effort and time. Stretching will help you relax and perform better; it will also help you relax and sleep better. Stretching is a good, practical way to learn and use muscle relaxation skills, and will be useful to you whether you are attending a business conference or riding in a three-day event.

Stretches for Specific Areas:

Shoulders and Neck   Shoulder rolls, arm circles.

Do them slowly, concentrate, feel the muscles stretch and the joints move freely.

Waist   Slow side bends. Feel the pull, count to eight, straighten slowly, repeat. *Crunches* will also help (see next entry).

Most of us have weak midsections and depend on our backs to do the work that should be done by our abdominals. This carries over to our riding. Instead of bracing our abdominal muscles to perform half-halts, for example, we use our backs.

Lower Back and Abdomen   Crunches, both straight and twisting. Twisting crunches will strengthen the sides of the waist, which will help protect you against sudden movements of a horse—shying, for instance.

The basic exercise to strengthen your lower back and abdominal muscles is the pelvic tilt. This is also the starting point for a number of other helpful exercises, and it is an essential exercise for riders, especially if you need to sit a horse's trot. To perform a basic pelvic tilt, first lie on your back with your knees bent, your feet on the floor, and your arms at your sides. There will be a hollow between your lower back and the floor—test this by sliding your hand in between the two. To perform the pelvic tilt, you tighten your abdominals, tilt your hips towards the ceiling, and push your lower back down towards the floor. Count five, relax, and begin again.

For basic crunches, begin with the pelvic tilt. With your lower back pushed down towards the floor, curl your upper body (head and shoulders) off the floor with your arms stretched straight out in front of you. Don't bounce, or pump with your arms. Hold for a count of five, return, and begin again. When this becomes easy for you, incorporate a slight twist of your torso to left or right as you curl up off the floor. For a useful variation on this exercise, put a chair in front of you and rest your calves on the chair. Do your crunches from this position, and when it becomes easy, do them the same way—but without the chair.

Back   To loosen and supple a stiff, tight lower back, lie flat on your back with your legs bent and your feet on the floor. Lift one leg towards your chest and try to touch your chest with your knee; then hold the ankle with one hand, and the thigh just above the knee with the other, and try to touch your knee to your chest AND your heel to your opposite hip. Anything you do to strengthen your abdominals and lower back will help you in your riding.

Thigh Adductors   The inside leg from crotch to knee is the area that typically becomes stiff and sore within a day of your weekly ride. To stretch this area, lie down, back flat, legs in the air, feet together. Separate your legs slowly until you feel the pulling sensation in the inner thigh, then stop and hold that position for a count of five, and put your legs slowly back together. Relax and repeat. One may be enough to begin with, but try to build up to ten repetitions. The key to this exercise is the *gentle* stretch and hold.

Hamstring and Knees Stretch   Sit on the floor, bring your feet together in front of you, and clasp them together with your hands. Keep your knees out to the sides, bent and pointing outward. Try to touch the floor with your knees: press them downwards very gently and slowly. Stop when it hurts or when the stretch becomes impossible, count to five, relax, and begin again. The farther your knees are from the floor, the more helpful this can be. The stretching is what matters, *not* how far down your knees go. Don't force them or bounce them. You can increase the amount of stretch by holding for longer counts, then by bringing your feet closer to your body.

To continue stretching thighs and add a gentle back stretch, hold your feet, keeping your knees down, and lean forward to touch the floor with your forehead. Again, take a slow, gentle approach with no bouncing. Eventually you may be able to hold your feet in your crotch and rest both knees on the floor—but even if you never come close to that, the exercise will make your riding, and your after-ride days, more comfortable.

Knees   Stand close to a door or bedpost for support, hold it with one hand, and reach for the outside of your ankle with your other hand. Bring the heel up as far as you can, hold for a count of five, let it down slowly, repeat. As with the other exercises, stretch gently. Do this daily; after a week you will notice that your thighs and knees are more relaxed.

Calves   Riders spend a lot of their time thinking "heels down." But all too often, those heels come back up whenever a rider isn't making a conscious effort to push them down. If this happens to you, and an honest analysis of your riding position tells you that you are *not* trying to hold the saddle with your knees, then you have tight calf muscles. You will have to stretch them if you want to be able to drop those heels comfortably. Are your calf muscles tight? How tight? Here's how to find out: take off your shoes, and squat on the floor with your knees tucked into your armpits. If your heels come off the floor while you do this, your calf muscles are tight.

There are easy ways of stretching your calf muscles. At home, you can stand with the balls of your feet balanced on the edge of a large telephone directory, or whatever else is handy and solid. Bend your knees slightly to approximate your normal riding position, relax, and let your weight sink into your heels. Those bent knees are very important. If you try to do this exercise with a stiff, straight leg, you will become stiff and tense as you try to force your heels down. Relax and let your own weight do the gentle stretching that your calf muscles need. This is a useful hotel-room exercise because there are always telephone directories in hotel rooms.

Exercises in the Stable

The gentle stretching and bending you do while grooming your horse can help you warm up. It can also promote the even development of your body, especially if you make a conscious effort to work equally with each side of the body, bending and flexing on both sides of the horse.

Exercises on the Horse

If you have the opportunity, do exercises on the longe: arm rotations, toe touches, side bends, torso twists, and neck rolls can all be performed on horseback, and will help your riding. Your instructor will be able to suggest additional leg exercises designed to help open up your hip joints and let you sit more deeply in the saddle.

Spending a little time in a half-seat or two-point position each time you ride will help you develop a stronger, steadier leg. For the more experienced rider, other exercises in the saddle will be equally profitable. Correctly done transitions, lateral work, and sitting trot will all contribute to your balance and flexibility.

Special Needs

Cross-Country Riders

Cross-country riders have special exercise requirements. They need strength in particular areas, especially thighs, calves, and lower back. The cross-country rider needs to put in a lot of time working in a half-seat at all gaits. Begin by riding once around the arena at walk, trot, and canter; then twice, three times, and so on. When this becomes easy, add upward and downward transitions. When the transitions become easy, shorten your stirrup leathers and begin again. Repeat the pattern until your stirrups are higher than you would actually use them for cross-country riding. Each adjustment you make will change the demands on the muscles that keep your body in balance, and they will develop accordingly.

Weekend Riders

Weekend, occasional, and irregular riders also have special needs. They need to be able to ride comfortably and not suffer days of pain and stiffness after each ride. Weekend riders are at particular risk from muscle spasm (cramp), so stretching exercises are especially important. On non-riding days, and before and after each ride, these riders should stretch their upper and middle backs, their lower backs, the fronts and backs of their thighs (hamstrings and quads), and their calves (Achilles' tendon stretch). This stretching will not build strength or endurance, however, and they will need additional exercises if they wish to achieve a higher level of fitness.

Fitness and Weight

Fitness should be your main goal, but fitness is easier to achieve when your weight is reasonably close to normal for you. Think in terms of fat, not weight. If you are fit and muscular, you may be heavier than a larger person who carries more fat and less muscle tissue. If you ride easily and comfortably, and your endurance is good, don't push yourself to match the weight you see on the insurance charts. Those charts don't take muscle weight or individual differences into account. If you are comfortable with your body and your fitness level, don't ruin your health and fitness in an attempt to become thin. Your primary concern should be your *fitness*, not your weight on the scales.

Riding Injuries

Although the subject of injuries is an uncomfortable one, riding is a high-risk sport, and certain types of injuries are common among riders and horse-handlers. Head injuries are all too common among riders. Riders should always wear properly fitted, properly fastened, protective helmets that meet or exceed the current ASTM/SEI safety standards.

Many injuries to the extremities—fingers and toes—can be avoided if you use common sense. Save your fingers by keeping them closed when you ride. Save your toes by wearing boots, and by being hyper-aware of where your horse's feet are when you are leading him.

A fit body is less prone to injury and recovers faster. Fitness, caution, preparation, and a good safety routine add up to good protection.

Medication

Most riders know that drinking and riding is foolish: Judgment, balance, and steering are all impaired by alcohol. But alcohol is not the only chemical that can influence your riding. Your "usual" medications—whether prescribed or over-the-counter—may affect your riding as well. Antihistamines, for instance, can have a significant effect on your reflexes and your balance. Check your sinus or allergy medication: does the packet carries a warning about operating heavy machinery?

Drowsiness, nervousness, slowed reaction time, and lack of coordination will affect your riding.

Many adult riders take some form of regular medication. If you have several prescriptions, be aware of their interactions, both among themselves and with any non-prescription drugs you may be taking. Know your medications and their effects, singly and collectively; this knowledge may have a real impact on your safety and that of your horse. If you are taking riding lessons and you have a physical or medical problem, or are recovering from an illness or an accident, tell your instructor *before your ride*. The information may affect any number of things: the horse that is selected, the tack that is used, and the plan for the lesson itself.

Slow Conditioning for Best Results

Give your own fitness program the same sort of planning and care that you would give a conditioning program for your horse. You wouldn't take an unfit horse out of a pasture and plunge him into a demanding exercise program; you wouldn't expect him to start in at the level of exercise that was appropriate when he was fit and strong, and you wouldn't take his exercise to the point of pain.

As your fitness program progresses, your muscles will develop and strengthen first; results will be visible in a matter of weeks. Bone takes longer to remodel and strengthen; this happens over a period of about six months. Tendons and ligaments, those all-important supporting structures, are the slowest to respond; these will strengthen slowly, over a year or longer.

Create a sensible program for yourself and take it slowly. Don't punish yourself for being unfit or for being less well-conditioned than you once were. Don't punish your body for not being as strong and agile as you think it should be, and above all, don't punish it for not being seventeen.

Fitness Is Achievable

As a child, you could probably do physical things almost instantly, as soon as you were told what to do. As an adult, and especially if your level of fitness is low, you will probably experience some frustration in learning to deal with the physical aspects of riding. Your adult body is stiffer, your reflexes are slower, and even when you understand what to do and how to do it, your body won't always respond instantly. When you do get the response you want, you may not be able to sustain the effort—or position, or action—for very long. Don't give up!

Take the trouble to improve your fitness level, or to maintain it if it is already good. Both you and your horse will appreciate your strength, endurance, flexibility, and coordination. As your fitness increases, your confidence and efficiency will improve, and so will your riding. Achieving and maintaining a correct position will be easier, your upper body will become more independent of your lower body, and your aids will become more clear and definite.

The process of physical conditioning is slow, but the payoff is very real. And there is one more advantage for you: your new understanding of fitness, conditioning, and strength training will enable you to give a long, detailed lecture to the very next person who is foolish enough to suggest to you that "the horse does all the work."

Finding the Right Instructor

If you are a beginning rider, your progress will be determined by the quality of your lessons. When you become an intermediate rider, your lessons will keep you on track and teach you more about the theory and techniques of riding. And even when you reach the advanced stage, you will still need a coach to help you enhance and refine your skills. Lessons, therefore, are all-important. If your finances and schedule will permit, you should take at least a weekly lesson with a good instructor. But how can you find the right instructor for you?

The obvious method would be for you to select your specialty of choice: jumping, dressage, eventing, or whatever your preference might be. Then, within that specialty, you would look for instructors. It's a simple method, and it doesn't always work.

What if nobody in your area teaches the specialty that most interests you? What if the best teacher in your area specializes in dressage, whereas your interest is in jumping? What if the local jumping instructor is not a good teacher?

If you are a beginning rider and can't find a suitable instructor within your chosen specialty, try to find someone capable and thorough who will start you off with good all-purpose basics: horse care, groundwork, and an all-purpose, balanced seat.

Carolyn Pribble, 50, Director of International Programs, College of Commerce, University of Illinois.

"I had ridden western most of my life, but I wanted to start again, and learn dressage. I hadn't ridden in a long time, and I wanted to do things differently. Things are different now: horses are better trained, and riders are better trained. I knew I needed to learn to ride properly and communicate with my horse, and it was clear to me that I didn't know how. I was lucky to find someone in my area who taught dressage and who could teach me, teach my horse, and teach me to teach my horse!"

Before You Sign Up

Do not sign up for lessons with anyone unless you have met them, seen their school horses, and watched them teach. Remember that the best performers are not necessarily the best teachers. Even if they have certificates from three different countries, even if they compete internationally or are Olympic medal winners—watch them teach.

You can learn from good riders just by watching them ride, but many successful competitors couldn't teach anyone if their lives depended on it. Some are intuitive riders who can't explain how or why they do something, because they have never intellectualized it. Some have no interest in teaching, and some are inarticulate or can't explain their methods to anyone who isn't riding at precisely their level. On the other hand, there are many excellent teachers who are no longer performing, and many who can teach to a higher level than they can now ride.

Consider the level of the lesson, as well. Watch lessons that are relevant to your standard. The coach who is brilliant with international-level dressage riders may be less effective with beginners; the instructor who can coax even the most frightened novice over a small grid may not be able to help you with your Grand Prix jumper.

If you have "inherited" the horse of a child who left for college after making you promise not to sell Champion, you may find that the instructor who was wonderful with your talented, single-minded, prize-winning young equestrian is less wonderful with your middle-aged, overworked, over-scheduled, much-less-ambitious self. If your styles and goals are not compatible, the instructor should recommend someone who specializes in teaching novice adult riders, and you should part with no hard feelings on either side. But this is more easily done in theory than in practice. Most instructors, whether they teach full-time or as a sideline, truly believe that they can help anyone. They tend to be quick to accept students, and reluctant to let them go. Take the time to observe and evaluate before you sign on with anyone; it's much easier to approach someone about giving you lessons than it is to tell your instructor that you wish to discontinue lessons.

Instructor Certification

A number of groups and institutions offer instructor certification programs. If your prospective instructor is certified, you should find out by whom, and what it means. Some instructors have a Red Cross certificate; some have actual instructor certification. The United States Dressage Federation (USDF) and the American Riding Instructor Certification Program (ARICP) both offer certification, as does the Camp Horsemanship Association (CHA). The British Horse Society (BHS) also offers certification.

If certification is important to you, you should contact the various groups and familiarize yourself with their standards and requirements so that you will know what each of their certificates means. If you have no idea what a certificate signifies, you won't know what you can expect from an instructor who holds that certificate. For instance, if your instructor holds a certificate from the BHS, you should know the difference between BHSAI (Assistant Instructor), BHSII (Intermediate Instructor), and BHSI (Instructor). Each designation represents a different level of training. Certification is not a guarantee of quality instruction. Many good instructors are not certified, and some not-so-good ones *are* certified. But if you are familiar with the various programs offering certification and find that the content and style of one of them is particularly appealing, then you might want to look for an instructor who has been certified by that program. It isn't a guarantee, but it is a good starting point.

How to Recognize Good Instruction

For the advanced, knowledgeable, experienced rider, recognizing good instruction is not so difficult. Years of lessons and training have created a wealth of information that the advanced rider can draw on consciously or unconsciously, and on which her opinion can be based. But what about the beginner or intermediate rider?

The basic requirements are, or should be, the same for all instructors: a wealth of knowledge; an ability to communicate; and respect for their students, for the sport itself, and for the horses. But many people can vocalize "philosophically correct" theory without actually putting it into practice. How can an inexperienced rider know the difference between those who merely talk the talk and those who walk the walk?

You will need to rely on your powers of observation, which are more highly developed than you think. Give the same attention to instructor selection that you would to crossing a busy street. Before you make your decision, stop, look, and listen. There are a number of observations that can tell you much of what you will need to know in order to evaluate a prospective instructor.

Facilities and School Horses

If your instructor owns or manages a stable, you will know a lot about her just by evaluating the facilities. You will also have learned something from observing the condition and attitude of her school horses, and the safety and appropriateness of their tack.

School horses should be alert, friendly, clean, healthy, sound, and not too thin. They should live in clean and dry stalls, and be well-behaved in lessons—not robots, of course, but patient and tolerant. Their tack should be simple: saddles, bridles, and neckstraps. There should be no gadgets or exotic paraphernalia ("dressage" tie-downs, bicycle-chain bits). There should also be no creative abuse with apparently innocent equipment: a too-tight noseband, intended to keep a horse from opening his mouth, is *not* acceptable. A much-too-short standing martingale is no longer a standing martingale; it has become a tie-down, forcing the horse's head down instead of keeping it from being flung too high. Even if you find the facilities, horses, and tack merely adequate, if there is nothing really wrong anywhere, give the instructor a chance to demonstrate her professional skills.

Watch a Lesson

When you find someone who teaches the form of riding you want to learn, and who teaches it at your level, arrange to watch a lesson or two. Most instructors will be happy to let you observe. In order to get the best information on which to base your opinion of her teaching, watch a lesson at your level—and preferably a lesson given to an adult. If you plan to participate in group lessons, watch a group lesson. The riders and horses should appear safe and comfortable, they should be working at the same level, and there should be no more than four students in the group unless the instructor has an assistant.

Remember that beginners and advanced riders need constant attention and feedback, and will benefit most from private lessons. Intermediate students, who can benefit from sharing a lesson with peers, can work well in small groups as described above. If you plan to take semiprivate lessons, watch one; if you plan to take private lessons, watch a private lesson.

If the lesson is at your level, you should have some idea of what is going on. And even if you are an absolute beginner, you can still ask yourself some pertinent questions. Does the student look comfortable, confident, and safe? Does the horse? Does the student appear to understand and act on what the instructor is saying—does the instructor make herself clear? Does there seem to be a plan to the lesson? In other words, does what is happening seem to be random activity, or is there a progression? What is your impression of the student's behavior? Is she attentive and responsive? Is she wearing suitable clothing? How about the horse—is he clean, not terribly thin or fat, and seemingly well-cared-for? Is the tack clean and simple, and does it fit the horse? Does the horse look comfortable and happy, not distressed or confused?

Watch as the lesson begins. Is the instructor's attention focused on the students? Does she make a quick check of their tack and equipment and then begin the lesson, or does she wave them on to the rail to circle endlessly while she chats with someone else? Students can become very frustrated when they are ignored for the first fifteen minutes of their forty-five- or sixty-minute lesson. They owe their instructor the courtesy of being ready on time; the instructor owes them the same courtesy.

During the lesson, watch the student-teacher interaction, and try to form an idea of whether the instructor's style and personality will be compatible with yours. Will you benefit from working with this person? If it seems to you that the horse understands and is going well, and that you are learning just by watching, try to imagine yourself in the place of the student. If you can, keep watching. If you find yourself thinking how attentive this instructor is, how much her style appeals to you, and how well she communicates, you may have found your instructor. But arrange to take a trial lesson or two before you decide.

Instructor Selection Guidelines

Cost

What is the price per hour? Does it cover the lesson *and* the school horse, or will there be an additional charge for the use of the horse?

If you have or intend to purchase a horse of your own, ask what the instructor would charge for schooling your horse and for coaching you at a show. This information will help you budget more effectively.

Although price cannot be your only consideration, or even your main consideration, call the local stables and find out the typical range of prices for your area. Prices vary by region, by specialty, and even by stable, but you should get an idea of what would be a reasonable price for the sort of lessons you want. If a particular instructor charges much more or much less than others in your region, try to find out why. The better-informed you are, the more likely you are to spend your money wisely.

Specialty

If the instructor teaches only dressage and your main interest is in jumping, you may still be able to benefit from her instruction until you are well past the beginner stage. When in doubt, always begin with the best possible instructor.

If you find a good instructor who can teach you the basic skills you will need to learn—horse handling, stable management, and a balanced seat—go ahead and sign up for lessons. A good balanced seat is a good starting point. You won't be developing a "specialized" seat until later, and even if you want to jump, you will do better to learn your basics from a good dressage instructor than from a bad hunt-seat instructor. If you find a wonderful hunt-seat instructor a year from now, you will already have your basics and be ready to move on.

Teaching Style

As in everything else, styles vary. There are any number of teaching styles (teacher in front, hands-on, lecture-demonstration, explanation, question-and-answer, and so forth) and many different approaches to instruction. As an adult, you have been exposed to enough different teachers to know what approach makes you most comfortable. You may respond well to a holistic, introduction-to-the-horse approach; or you may be most comfortable with a touchy-feely, New Age approach, or even a linear-learning, first-we-do-A, then-we-do-B approach. Or you may be entirely at ease with someone whose style is purely military. Some students respond best to an intellectual/mental approach; others are more comfortable with a more physical/mechanical method. Still others are most comfortable with an instructor who approaches their training on an emotional or situational "feelings" level. Good instructors often use a combination of these approaches and can adapt their style to a student's needs.

No matter what their style, the best instructors will demonstrate experience, patience, effectiveness, imagination, and humor. They will not just issue orders but will explain concepts: reasons and causes, actions and reactions. The best instructors will teach from the horse's point of view, and will teach the students to follow the mental processes of the horse.

Attitude

Whatever style you may prefer, you will need an instructor whose attitude is positive and encouraging. If you find that a prospective instructor's attitude is negative and that a lesson consists of constant criticism, look elsewhere. This is supposed to be a positive, enjoyable experience for you and your horse. The good instructor will be prepared, consistent, and positive: her instructions to students will be affirmative rather than negative. This is all-important, as it affects the learning process itself: "DO this" is useful; "Don't do that" is not. If your instructor spends more time telling you *not* to do things than she does telling you to *do* things, you will learn much more slowly.

Students, like horses, need to be told—or shown—what, specifically, is wanted and how to do it. "Sit tall, open your chest, breathe" is useful; "Don't lean forward, don't hunch" is not. The instructor's obligation is to communicate effectively so as to build rider confidence while the student develops balance and harmony with the horse.

Communication

A good instructor will be able to get through to the student, even if it means saying the same thing in ten different ways. Communication has to be two-way. It isn't enough just to make a pronouncement—the process is not complete until the student understands. A good instructor will be sure of her subject, and will explain clearly and simply, one step at a time. She will be able to demonstrate, and will do most demonstrations from the ground, getting on the student's horse only *with permission* and as a last resort. A good instructor will be an accurate observer with a good "eye," will recognize imbalance and tension, and will provide exercises to correct these and other problems. She will be patient, clear, enthusiastic, and she will reward often. She will, in short, deal with students and horses in the same way.

Questions

Your instructor should encourage you to ask questions. If you ask at the wrong time—this happens—your instructor may say "Not now," but she should still respond, even if you have to wait for a break, or until the end of the lesson, for the answer. If an instructor makes fun of you or your questions, or gives you answers such as "That's just the way horses are" or "That's just the way we do this," think twice before booking another lesson (then book it with another instructor).

There are reasons for everything you will be asked to do. There is a reason for every position, a reason for every exercise, and a reason for every action. If you know the reasons behind the position or the exercise, you will be able to do it better. And when you work alone, between lessons, it will be easier for you to remember *what* you should do if you know *why* you should do it.

Planning and Flexibility

A good instructor will keep an eye on you as you warm up, and modify her lesson plan according to what she sees. She will review the previous lesson's teaching or training, teach with short- and long-term goals in mind, and keep profiles on students, outlining their progress.

Safety

A good instructor will be safety-oriented. She will have rules based on safety and on the proper handling and riding of horses, and she will enforce those rules across the board. At the very least, students will be required to wear safety helmets and boots, and will not be allowed to wear jewelry or chew gum. The rules will also apply to the instructor herself: if she gets on a student's horse to demonstrate a movement, she will put her helmet on first.

Position

A good instructor will be concerned with your position from the very beginning of your lessons. Position is not superficial; it is the basis for everything else you will learn. An incorrect position, whether of your head, arms, back, seat, legs, or feet, will have an effect on other body parts and create incorrect positions there also. A good instructor will not merely point out superficial position errors ("your heels are up") and suggest fixes ("push them down"), she will explain what is causing the error and why it is important that you fix it correctly. She will discuss causes, not just effects.

Ethics

A good instructor will be ethical, not just in her dealings with students but in her dealings with the animals in her care. An ethical instructor will not abuse or overuse lesson horses and will not frighten students by presenting them with tasks beyond their current abilities. It is the instructor's responsibility to interpret the horse to the rider and to enhance the rider's ability to communicate with the horse. It is also the instructor's responsibility to ensure that students act towards the horses with consideration and respect; the instructor must speak for the horses.

Role Model

Your instructor is your role model in several areas: she is your riding model, your horse-care model, and your behavior and attitude model. Good instructors never forget that they are role models; if they do something that seems to contradict their teachings, they will explain it. The best instructors don't "preach water and drink wine"—they live the values that they teach.

Equipment Safety Check

Although a good instructor will probably not groom and tack up the horses herself, she will take a few moments to inspect each horse and his tack at the beginning of the lesson—even if the horse is not hers, the tack is not hers, and the student is an experienced rider. This is not an insult to the student but a reflection of the fact that the instructor is responsible for the safety of horse and rider. This pre-ride check is the time to notice equipment problems: if the saddle flap on the off side is folded under itself, the girth is twisted, the saddle pad is pressing on the horse's withers, or the bridle is adjusted incorrectly, these problems should be dealt with before the lesson begins. This brief inspection will also allow the instructor to notice whether the student is correctly turned out, and to suggest readjusting the helmet, removing the jewelry, and disposing of the chewing gum.

Whether you are a beginner, an intermediate, or an advanced rider, in the interest of your own safety, and because it is good practice, you should learn to check your tack at the beginning of each ride. Look at the bridle: is the stitching intact? is the leather sound, or cracked? Pay particular attention to the area that curves around the bit. Check the stitching and the leather of the reins. Look at the saddle: lift the flaps on both sides, and check the billets. Is the stitching intact, is the leather sound, and are the holes round, or do they look more like slots—or tears? Check the stitching, the leather, the buckles, and the elastic (if any) on the girth. And while you are checking the tack, notice whether it fits the horse. This safety check takes only a moment to do, and it is worth doing *every time you ride.*

School Horses/Beginner Horses/ Horses for the Weekend Rider

Many adult riders, whether they are beginners or accomplished riders whose busy professional schedules don't allow them to ride very often, need a solid and dependable horse. Pretty is nice, but not essential. The horses used for adult lessons, especially adult beginner lessons, have to be horses with certain specific qualities.

Any school horse must be serviceably sound and reasonably well-trained, but that is not enough. School horses for adult beginners must be forgiving and patient. Children pull and kick and hang off their horses' sides, and their horses have to be patient, too, but in a different way. Adults are less casual, more careful—and more tense and fearful. Rider tension and fear are communicated instantly to the horse, who then becomes tense himself and eventually fearful as well.

As the horse becomes more tense and worried, he becomes less comfortable and predictable for the rider, who in turn becomes more tense and rigid, which affects the horse—and a potentially danger- ous, self-amplifying feedback loop is established. No real learning can take place in this situation. The only solution is to break the loop and eliminate the feedback, and the only way to achieve this is for the instructor to have access to an absolutely quiet, utterly reliable, generous, understanding, forgiving school horse.

Such solid-gold horses do exist, but they tend to be older, unglamorous beasts, many of whom are on regular medication to maintain their precarious soundness. There is nothing wrong with this, but it brings out another difference between children and adults. Children, who may not need to learn on this sort of a horse, are perfectly happy to ride anything with four legs and a tail. To the beginner child, all horses are beautiful and exciting, and to sit on a moving animal is an indescribable thrill. The beginner adult is often less easy to please. Adults tend not to appreciate the sort of horse they actually need; they prefer younger, more attractive, infinitely less suitable horses, and have been known to complain when presented with what they see as a "plodder." But for adult beginners, who need to relax, become more supple, and learn to move with the horse instead of perching awkwardly on top of him, this sort of horse is ideal.

On such a horse, adult beginners can learn relaxation and confidence. They can make mistakes, sit badly, give incorrect signals, and then learn to do better, all without upsetting the horse and causing tension that makes it impossible for the rider to stay relaxed, let alone achieve a feeling of confidence. Regardless of their innate abilities and the skills of their instructor, their progress through relaxation and confidence to proficiency will depend on their learning basic skills on a horse that will look after them.

Later on, when their basic skills have become second nature, and they are able to sit correctly and give aids deliberately, when they are directing the horse's movements rather than simply following them, they will be able to try out their new skills by attempting to make those school horses more responsive to the aids.

Still later, it will be useful for those riders to ride other horses that will react to their mistakes instead of simply carrying on. And eventually, once the adults become proficient and wish to purchase their own horses, they will not need to look for quiet, reliable horses like the ones that taught them their basics. But without such horses to ride in the beginning stages, those riders may never become proficient, because they cannot acquire the basic skills of riding if they are tense and fearful and if all their attention is focused on one thing: staying on.

Warning Signs of Bad Instruction

Beware of the horse-as-machine approach to riding and training: *"There's a gadget for every problem"; "A new bit (or martingale) will fix that horse."* Beware of anyone whose only approach to problem-solving involves adding more equipment, or more severe hardware. Equipment problems (a saddle that pinches or a bit with a sharp edge) can and should be solved with different equipment. Training problems, on the other hand, cannot and should not be dealt with on a mechanical basis.

Beware of the horse-as-adversary approach to riding and training: *"He's just trying to get out of work"* does not explain a lameness, and *"Don't let him get away with that"* is not a universal response to a horse's failure to respond as expected.

Beware of dictators: *"Don't question my methods"; "I know what I'm doing."* Your job as a student is to collect information, and you must be able to ask questions and have them answered properly and completely. *"Because I say so"* is never a good reason.

Beware of the tough approach: *"You can't hurt a horse"; "It's too far from the heart to kill him."* It may seem logical to think that a horse is so large and strong-looking that there is nothing you could possibly do which would hurt him—not so. Horses may be big, but many of their systems are more delicate than you would imagine.

And, lastly, beware of the flatterers: Withhold your trust from any instructor, or any clinician, who tells you that you are a fabulous natural rider and that you have only one problem: your horse. This sort of blarney (*"You could be a top rider, but your horse is holding you back"*) may warm the hearts of the gullible, but stop and think. There is a reason for this nonsense, but it isn't that this clever, perceptive person is absolutely overwhelmed by your raw talent. You are simply being set up to believe that you would be riding in the next Olympic Games if you could just get your hands on the sort of horse you deserve—something like, well, that Swedish Warmblood gelding the instructor or clinician just happens to have for sale. This doesn't mean that horses never hold back their riders, but in almost all cases it is actually the other way around. Use your judgment, and when you hear something along those lines, consider the source before you act.

Your regular instructor, who is familiar with your status, progress, goals, and desires, will be able to help you evaluate your situation. When your trusted instructor of several years points out that ol' Big Ears is getting stiff and slowing down and that if you want to win over 4' fences (or at Third Level dressage) you might want to start thinking about a new horse, *that* will be the time to begin your search.

Paying Your Dues

Beware of instant anything: nothing about riding or training will benefit from a hurried approach. Save time by taking your time. Beware of anyone promising shortcuts: good riding takes time, attention, and mileage. Notice that I don't say talent, because talent certainly helps, but it doesn't guarantee that the person who possesses it will become a good rider. If you want to be a good rider and a horseman, you must accept the fact that you will have to pay your dues. There are no shortcuts and no secret formulas for quick success. Riding is more than a physical skill; it is an art.

Talent without drive will get nowhere, talent and drive will go just about anywhere, and, oddly enough, drive without talent can go far. Motivation is not enough—it will get you started, but it's determination that will see you through. And just like the rest of real life, if something sounds too good to be true, it probably is.

A Final Word on Instructors

Like the ideal horse, the ideal instructor probably doesn't exist. But you should know what qualities the ideal instructor should possess, just as you should know what qualities the ideal horse should possess. Whether you are searching for a horse, an instructor, or both, you should be able to determine what your absolute requirements are and what faults you can forgive.

A good instructor will teach you enough so that you will eventually be able to school the horse or teach him something new even if your instructor isn't there—after all, that's the point. Once you have learned what you are doing and what the horse is doing, you will be able to work more and more on your own. The instructor who held your hand and took you step by step through the first stages can now step back and become a coach—still there when you need her but not directing your every move. A good instructor's goal should be to help you help yourself, not to make you completely and perpetually dependent on her.

A good instructor will help you save time and avoid many costly, time-consuming, frustrating, and dangerous mistakes. Finding a good instructor will also help you save money, as you will not be wasting it on poor-quality instruction. Good instruction will help you to become and stay fit. It will also help your horse to become fitter and stay sound. A good instructor will teach horsemanship as well as riding: students will learn horse handling, horse care, grooming, conditioning, and more. A good instructor will not assume that students come with the correct basics, even if they have had lessons before.

A good instructor will bring out the best in you and will know when to encourage you, when to push you, and when to back off. She will design a program for you that is based on your physical condition and your goals, and which takes into account your schedule and obligations. A good instructor is a formative influence, regardless of your age or experience. Your relationship with your instructor is the single most important influence in the development of your riding skills and your attitude towards horses. What you learn from your instructor will have a tremendous effect on your relationship with your horse.

The Art of Taking Lessons

Adult riders need lessons aimed at adults. You already know how to learn, you have a longer attention span than you had as a child, and you are motivated to learn.

You already know that the first priority of any good instructor will be safety. Safety means more than helmets and boots—it means education.

The cause of most difficulties with horses—and accidents around them—is riders' and handlers' ignorance of how horses work physically and mentally. Adult riders should learn enough about horses to know what their normal behavior is, as well as which practices are safe, both on the ground and in the saddle. An instructor whose primary focus is teaching equitation for the show ring is the wrong teacher for an adult. You will need to learn horsemanship, not just riding.

Your First Lessons: What to Expect

Your first lessons should involve little time on horseback and much time learning about horse anatomy, behavior, handling, grooming, and tack. This is time well-spent.

Paige Miller, 28, single (engaged), attorney.
"I try to take a lesson every week. Lessons keep me on track and give me
something to work for."

Groundwork

You may have to ask or encourage your instructor to spend the first few lessons covering the basics on the ground. Many instructors may worry that students will feel "cheated" if they don't spend all of every lesson on the horse's back.

When you begin spending most of your lesson in the saddle, it will take time for you to learn the basics of position and seat. The main consideration during early mounted lessons will be your position. Nothing will interfere with your progress more than errors in basic position. Most beginner-rider problems—and many problems of more advanced riders—are the direct result of incorrect position.

Work on the Longe

If your instructor begins with longe lessons, you have a good chance to learn correct posture and relaxation. On the longe, you can become familiar with the horse's movements and learn to maintain your position and adjust your balance as the horse moves. You will be able to focus entirely on yourself, without having to be responsible for controlling the horse's gait, direction, or speed.

The ideal way to begin: on the longe line.

Your first mounted lessons should be short: half an hour will be quite enough for the first few sessions. Before you ride, warm up thoroughly and do your stretching exercises. Do them again before bed—you will still be sore the next day, but not too sore to move.

Getting the Most from Your Lessons

A good riding instructor is a knowledgeable and articulate person, able to interpret horse to rider and vice versa. By taking lessons from such a person, you will acquire the skills you desire. But beware of counting too much on your instructor and too little on yourself. Taking lessons is an active process, not a passive one. Your full participation is required. You cannot just relax and be taught. Ask yourself whether you are "taking" lessons or whether you are expecting your instructor to "give" you lessons.

Lessons are the key to progress, and we know how to take lessons— or do we? Riding lessons, for adults, are often a gift we give ourselves. We schedule them, take them, pay for them, but are we truly getting all we can get from them? To get the most from our lessons, we must understand what elements are involved in a lesson, and how the various obligations and responsibilities are divided among the participants.

The basic requirements for both instructor and student are respect for the animal, respect for the human, and respect for the discipline. We expect more from our instructor: a thorough knowledge of the discipline; a solid understanding of horsemanship; an accurate appreciation of the physical, mental, and emotional characteristics of her pupils, equine and human; and the ability to make herself understood quickly, clearly, and without violence.

But there are three parties to any lesson: instructor, student, and horse. All three must be able to communicate with one another. During each lesson, the instructor is responsible for the actions and progress of both student and horse; between lessons, the student is responsible for the actions and progress of herself and the horse. The student's obligations are to derive as much benefit as possible from the time spent with the instructor and to make constructive use of the time between lessons.

You Can Improve Your Lessons

If you come to each lesson prepared mentally, physically, and emotionally, you will get the most for your money and maximize the benefit to yourself and your horse. Unlike a dressage test, which allows the judge to evaluate your riding and your horse's training in just a few minutes, a lesson allows you to have your riding critiqued, corrected, changed, and critiqued again. Your instructor can introduce you to something new or drill you in a basic skill until it becomes automatic. Your instructor may be helping you stay balanced during your first walk-trot transition, or she may be functioning as a coach, reminding you to sit tall and not allow yourself to collapse over your inside hip in half-pass. Regardless of your level of skill, the basic requirements of lesson-taking are the same. Most of your obligations and responsibilities are simple matters of courtesy and practicality; all of them are within your reach.

Be on Time for Your Lesson   "On time" doesn't mean swinging into the driveway at the last possible moment, gears clashing and gravel flying. "On time" means on your horse, warmed up and stretched, ready to go when the instructor arrives. Respect the schedule, even if you are a lucky student whose instructor is willing and able to stretch the lesson past the "official" time. A student who is tacking up—or arriving—when her lesson begins may lose five or ten minutes before she even mounts. Once she's mounted, she will need to warm up. Even five minutes of tacking up and ten minutes of warming up will make a large hole in a one-hour lesson.

Dress Correctly and Safely   This doesn't mean show turnout, but your clothing should allow you to ride to the best of your ability and should not interfere with your instructor's view of you. Don't wear loose, billowing shirts, baggy jeans that make folds under your knees, or rubber boots that dig into the front of your ankles when you drop your weight into your heels.

Do wear show clothes if you are preparing for a show and have something new to wear. If your new breeches or boots are going to interfere with your performance by restricting your movement or flexibility—and believe me, this has happened to all of us—find out at your lesson, not at the show.

Have Your Horse Dressed Correctly   Show tack is not necessary, but come to your lesson with clean, properly fitted tack on a reasonably clean horse. Again, if you are preparing for a competition, this is the time to try out the new bridle, saddle, bit, or even stirrup leathers. Don't change your equipment the night before a show. You will suffer through your class, over your course, or through your test, wondering why you are behind your leg or why your horse is shaking his head. Try your new equipment at home, in a lesson, before you take it on the road.

Be Prepared: Physically, Mentally, and Emotionally   Physical preparation need not be elaborate, although the stronger and more supple your body, the better your physical responses will be. You *should* be fit enough to take a lesson: you won't get much out of it if you are suffering from tight tendons, sore muscles, and shortness of breath. Mental preparation need not be elaborate either. Be ready for your lesson: know what you have worked on since your last lesson, and be prepared to *listen.*

Remember that you are there to learn. If your instructor is also a friend and you feel a need to chat and catch up, arrange to have coffee afterward, or plan to go out to lunch at another time. Keep your lesson as businesslike as possible.

A good instructor will be more interested in your progress than in her own ego and will be more concerned with gaining your respect than gaining your friendship. Even if your instructor is one of your very dearest friends, you will benefit more from your lesson if you keep to business. It is easier to give (and take) needed criticism in a professional atmosphere. Offer your regular instructor the same respect and careful attention that you would give an expensive clinician from out of town.

Emotional preparation is simple: be ready to do your best and change what needs changing. Your instructor is there to help you. Her criticisms are constructive; they are offered without malice and should not be taken personally. It's your leg or arm position that's being criticized, not your personal worthiness.

Realize that even the most caring, understanding, and compassionate instructor will occasionally push or challenge you. One of the duties of an instructor is to push you a little harder than you want to be pushed and take you a little farther than you want to go—not always, not all the time, but sometimes.

If the "push" is done well, you should go home a little bit frightened and very excited and pleased, having successfully confronted your first extended trot, your first four-foot fence—or your first solo off the longe line. Good instructors can make their students stretch themselves without frightening, insulting, or confusing them.

Realize also that even the most caring, understanding, and compassionate instructor can have an "off day." This should not happen often; one of the hallmarks of a good instructor is her ability to separate professional from personal life and to give students her full attention even if her personal life is crashing around her. But she will occasionally, rarely, have an "off day," and you will need to work harder to keep the lesson on track.

Maximizing Your Money's Worth

Use Your Time Wisely As soon as you are able to prepare for the lesson yourself, arrive early enough to catch, groom, tack up, and warm up your horse at a walk for ten or fifteen minutes before your lesson actually begins. The time you pay for will then be spent on the riding lesson itself and not on tacking up or warming up. You will get more from your lessons if you do everything you can on your own time.

Avoid Confusion You will get more from your lessons by avoiding confusion. Avoid contracting clinic syndrome, the cause of which is listening to too many clinicians, and the main symptom of which is inconsistency on the part of the rider. Clinic syndrome is largely based on confusion. When a rider tries to learn too many systems, changing every week or two according to the last authority consulted, she becomes inconsistent with her horse—and eventually ineffectual.

If you have a good instructor, don't waste your money or your time "shopping around." There are many systems of riding and training; give yourself the chance to learn one of them thoroughly. Trying to learn three different systems simultaneously won't make you three times the rider. Your instructor won't be able to help you as effectively if you are learning her system on Mondays and two other systems on Wednesdays and Fridays. Find a good instructor, and then stay with her until you find either the instructor or the system unsatisfactory.

Make the Effort; Go the Distance   You can't benefit from a lesson you don't take. If you have scheduled a lesson and can get there on time, go. Your instructor—you selected an instructor who understands the needs and problems of adults, remember?—won't embarrass you or frighten you by asking you to do something that is beyond your level of fitness or ability. Consider the following scenarios.

> **Scenario 1**   *You haven't ridden since your last lesson, and you think you shouldn't bother with this lesson either since you aren't prepared.*
>
> Go to your lesson, ride your horse, listen to your instructor. Don't underestimate the effectiveness of latent learning—sometimes you have a wonderful lesson after you've had some time away.
>
> This works for your horse, too. Sometimes, after ten minutes of warming up, your horse will volunteer the movement you had just begun to attempt two weeks ago, before things went crazy at the office and you had to stay late every night. Your horse can exhibit latent learning, and so can you.

> **Scenario 2**   *You are having such a bad time with your riding lately that you feel hopeless, and you really don't want your instructor to see you when you're such a disaster.*
>
> Leave your ego in the tack room and get on that horse. If you will give it an honest try, your instructor should be able to help you work through your difficulties. Good instructors have huge repertoires of exercises designed to help specific problems. Let your instructor help you.
>
> Lessons are intended to help you improve, and sometimes a bad day can bring on a wonderful lesson. If you put your very worst problems out for your instructor to see, she will be able to determine what you need, and help you. If you wait until you feel "just right," you won't have many lessons, and you won't improve.

> **Scenario 3**   *You're just back from five days of sick leave, and you still feel weak.*
>
> Tell your instructor. We've all given lessons at the walk and halt—and students have learned a lot without hurting or stressing themselves, and gone home happy.

Scenario 4 *Your instructor raised the jumps to 3'3" at your last lesson, and although your horse made it over all of them, you didn't feel that you were really in control. Now you're looking for excuses not to take your lesson or, at least, not to jump.*

Tell your instructor how you felt, how you feel now, and ask how she can help you develop more confidence. Again, any good instructor can reach down into that bag of exercises and pull out four or five designed to make you feel more comfortable and more in control of your horse and your situation.

How Your Instructor Thinks

Here are a few insights into the way your instructor thinks. Yes, instructors do have peeves—but they may not be what you expected! Here are some that many of us share:

- The student who has plenty of time, but never rides in between lessons, and shows little or no progress as a result. (*Note*: this does *not* apply to students who actually don't have time to ride.)

- The student who is never on time for a lesson, but expects the instructor to give her the full hour anyway.

- The student who is so unfit that she literally cannot stay on her horse for the duration of the lesson, or worse, whose horse is obviously not fit enough to last through an entire lesson. The worst possible variation on this theme is the student who comes in on a lame horse and demands her lesson anyway.

- The student who dresses so sloppily that her riding and the instructor's view of her are both impaired (for example, the student wearing loose jeans and a billowy anorak, or a size 3X t-shirt on a size 12 body). Students who dress appropriately make their riding easier and show respect for themselves, their instructors, and the sport.

- The student who talks constantly: either chatting and gossiping, or arguing. You can't listen and talk at the same time.

- The student who refuses to try, either because she thinks she is inadequate or because she thinks her horse is. She spends more time apologizing for imagined shortcomings than she does working on her riding.

- The student who takes out her frustration and temper on her horse—this is the antithesis of horsemanship, and cannot be accepted by any good instructor.

- The student who seems to understand, and who performs better over the course of each lesson, but obviously returns to her previous mode of riding in between lessons, makes no real progress, and requires to be taught the same things over and over again.

Notice that *nowhere* in the list appears the student who is too old, the student who is too heavy, the student who isn't a "natural," or the student who is "just a beginner."

Note also that there is no mention of the horse; students tend to worry that their horse isn't big enough or fancy enough or a flashy enough mover, or that he is the "wrong" breed.

So don't worry. These things don't matter to us (unless you have announced that you are planning to go to the Olympics with that particular horse). What does matter to us is helping you become the best rider you can be, and helping you to train your horse to be the best horse he can be. Consistent instruction will make you a better rider and will help you make your horse a better horse. Any horse can be improved. Too many horses are sold on because their owners have inaccurate perceptions of their own riding skills and of their horses' potential.

Students often sabotage their lessons and their learning without even being aware that they have done so. Sometimes this self-sabotage comes from a misunderstanding about what they can expect from their horse or their instructor; more often, it comes from a misunderstanding about what they should expect from themselves. Clear, honest communication between instructor and student can usually eliminate such misunderstandings. If you feel that you simply aren't riding well, or if your schedule has been so hectic that your riding time between lessons has been limited to once around the arena at the walk, on the only evening you were in town, tell your instructor. She can tailor your lesson to your state of preparation, or to your level of fitness or health. Don't spend the whole lesson apologizing, but do let her know what your situation is. She will not be angry or upset or disappointed in you.

Time Out

If you need a break during a lesson, or if you feel that your horse needs a break, ask for time out. If you have left it too late to say anything—if you suddenly realize that your leg or your horse's neck is beginning to cramp, for example—just drop your reins, stretch, take a moment to relax your muscles. You won't have to do a lot of explaining; your instructor will understand.

Sometimes it is useful for you to prolong an exercise past the point of comfort, just to build your endurance. This might mean staying in a two-point position until you are sure you can't possibly stay there any longer, then making yourself count ten more strides before you sit. Or it might mean continuing to use your legs actively, once more all the way around the arena, when you are quite sure that they are going to fall off at any moment. But there is a moment at which the exertion becomes too painful or too exhausting, and this is when you need to *stop* or *change* what you are doing. If you persist past this point, the stress and discomfort will cause you to ride badly or your horse to move badly—which are completely counterproductive.

You must be aware of your body and know whether your legs are telling you "We don't want to do any more of this" or "We *can't* do any more of this." And you must also be aware of your horse's body, and his ability to continue performing an exercise, so that you don't push him to the point of cramping or pain. Your relationship with your equine partner will be much more pleasant, and your horse will trust you much more, if you know when to stop or change what you are doing—and if you do it before your horse becomes unhappy with you, with the movement, and with the whole idea of being ridden.

A good instructor will build regular breaks and stretches into any lesson, but sometimes an exercise can go on just a little too long. When this happens, you must act on behalf of yourself or your horse. Don't keep pushing until you stop breathing and stiffen and do something that will hurt you or your horse. Instead, call "Time out"; do a nice, balanced transition down to the walk; slip the reins to your horse so that he can relax and stretch; and then breathe deeply and let your own body relax.

Instructors often become enthusiastic when students and horses are performing well or are just on the brink of understanding a new concept or movement, and sometimes we push a little too hard or for a little too long. Your instructor cannot always know the precise moment when you reach the point of fatigue or pain, but you will know, and you can do something about it.

Self-Improvement

In addition to private or group lessons, there are a number of ways to supplement your formal instruction. In a previous chapter, you learned various ways to enhance or improve your physical fitness. There are other ways you can help yourself and your riding, according to the amount of time and money you can afford to invest.

More Money than Time

If you have plenty of money but less time than you would like, you should take private lessons, attend clinics, buy the best videos and watch them, buy the best books and read them. Have someone videotape your own lessons, and watch them at home. If you drive to work, listen to instructional audio cassettes in your car.

Some Money, Some Time

If you have less money but more time, take as many lessons as you can afford to. Watch as many lessons as you possibly can. You will learn a lot, and you will also be training yourself to see more accurately. The same applies to clinics. If a three-day clinic is offered and you can only afford to ride during one session, you can still learn from the entire clinic. Pay an auditing fee for the other sessions if one is charged, but by all means be there and watch carefully.

Think of the time you spend watching lessons and clinics as an investment—it will be, if you learn from what you see. You may learn techniques that you and your instructor can try out on your own horse. At the very least, you will learn whether you want to take lessons or a clinic with this person, and whether her approach suits you. Save money by not spending it foolishly; watch and learn before you buy.

Read everything. Books are expensive, and sometimes the contents don't live up to the title, so take a tip from horsemen and try before you buy. Of course you will want to have your own collection of reference books, but do a lot of reading the inexpensive way before you decide what you want to purchase.

Your public library has at least a few books on horses, riding, and horse training, and what they don't have they can get for you via interlibrary loan. And watch good riding whenever you can. This will often mean watching videos, whether they are bought, rented, or borrowed. Buy only those videos that you want most. There are more time-consuming ways of arranging to see the others: you may, for instance, arrange swaps with fellow students, riders, or boarders; you may also join one of the horse-video clubs and rent tapes.

More Time than Money

Lesson prices can vary; it may be possible for you to negotiate a discount for a book of lessons paid for—or even signed for—in advance. And if you can't arrange a discount, consider some of the following suggestions.

Exchanging Your Professional Skills for Lessons Consider the barter system. Even today, barter is still possible: exchange your services for something you want. Something you do well in your professional or personal life may be valuable to the owner of your boarding stable or to your instructor. Try bartering your skills for board or lessons. The stable owner or your instructor might be interested in your skills as a writer (you might create brochures, advertisements, or show bills) or as a carpenter (you might build jumps, mounting blocks, tack trunks, cavalletti). If you are a cook or caterer, you may be able to exchange food for lessons. If you can create something that someone else wants—art, pottery, or a hand-knit sweater—you may ready to barter. Whether you design jewelry, train dogs, clean houses, or repair cars, whatever you do in the "real" world may be something you can exchange for lessons, stall space, or other services.

Moonlighting and Freelancing   Alternatively, you might choose to use your professional skills elsewhere. A bit of freelancing in your own field, for instance, might bring in money that you could use for your horse activities. If you have a useful marketable skill, it may be more cost-effective to earn your lesson money in this way than to spend twice or three times as many hours doing barn chores.

Helping with Lessons   Many instructors are kept quite busy with the teaching part of their duties. You may be able to work off your own lessons by helping with other lessons. This could mean grooming horses and tacking up, it could mean assisting with lessons by serving as jump crew, it could mean helping to mow or paint fences or build jumps, or it could mean watering or raking the dressage arena.

Barn Chores   If you review your professional skills and discover nothing that would be useful, you may still be able to work off your lessons or board. There are certain constants in the horse world, and one of these is the infinite renewability of barn chores. There is always work to be done at every stable: sweeping aisles, cleaning water buckets, removing cobwebs, fixing fences, feeding horses, grooming horses, and, yes, mucking out. These chores are perpetual: No matter what sort of stable it is or what sort of horses live there, those horses must be fed and watered and their stalls must be cleaned every day.

Don't make the mistake of imagining that these tasks are suitable only for menials and eager, ignorant adolescents. This is simply untrue. There is nothing even slightly demeaning about mucking out; it is a necessary part of horse care and stable maintenance, and it has to be done every day at every barn. The true horseman doesn't despise any job associated with caring for horses. No one should be too proud to muck out a stall, although I have heard adults insist that "that sort of work" is beneath them, even if the horse is their own. They are wrong, and I certainly hope that they are never left alone with a baby in need of a diaper change!

But the fact that some people think this way means that there are always stalls to muck out, if you are willing to do the work. And although barn chores do not generally pay well, there is something deeply satisfying about knowing that the horses are benefiting immediately and directly from what you are doing.

Advantages of "Doing" Your Own Horse

If one of the horses you look after is your own, you will find that there are practical advantages associated with caring for your own horse. The person who feeds and grooms her horse and mucks out his stall has a much more accurate understanding of his normal eating and drinking habits, his usual rate of salt consumption, and his hay and grain preferences, than does the owner who can afford full-service board.

The hands-on owner's familiarity with the normal habits of her horse means that she has a system in place to monitor her horse's health. This owner will be quick to notice warning signs of stress or illness in her horse. Slower eating, a usually empty bucket still full of water in the morning, changes in the color or texture of the manure, or a stall that shows signs of having been rolled in extensively overnight—these are all early warning signals that might be missed by someone who comes out only to ride.

This is not the only advantage of "doing" your own horse. Looking after all the needs of your animal builds an understanding and a relationship between you. People whose schedules or inclinations allow them barely enough time to ride, and no time to work around or socialize with their horses, cannot achieve this same closeness with their animals. The horse in a stall is an animal in an artificial environment, and like an infant, he is totally dependent on humans for his basic necessities: food, water, salt, clean bedding, companionship, and affection. If you, personally, are able to provide some or all of these necessities, your horse will come to regard you as a very good friend indeed.

Rewards of Looking after Horses

Looking after a number of horses can be a very rewarding experience. Even if your goal in feeding all the horses and mucking out four stalls every morning is to work off the cost of your own horse's board, you can't help but be pleased when you see a horse lie down and roll luxuriously in the clean bedding you have placed in his stall, or take a long, satisfying drink of the cool water with which you have just filled his bucket. It can be difficult to leave your warm bed on a frosty morning so that you can get to the stable before sunrise, feed ten or twenty or forty horses, and get to the office on time. But again, beyond the knowledge that this extra work enables you to keep your own horse at the stable of your choice, you will feel great satisfaction when you enter the stable and see every head turned towards you and hear the horses greeting you.

Warning

If you do stable chores, you and the stable owner or instructor should agree in advance, *preferably in writing*, on the rate of exchange, and determine exactly how many hours of what sort of work will be required for you to earn a weekly lesson or pay for your horse's board. If there is confusion about how long certain chores should take, or how many hours of chores represent one lesson or one month's board, the arrangement can become complicated and unpleasant, with resentment on both sides. On the other hand, if both parties define their terms and hammer out an agreement in advance, keep track of all hours worked, all board covered, and all lessons given, the experience can be a pleasant one.

Watch and Learn

There are other ways to advance your riding education. Spend some time watching other people take lessons. Watch the instructor teach, see how much you can understand of what is being said and how it is being understood and how well it works.

If you can't afford to ride in a clinic, remember that you can learn a lot from watching. Don't stay home—go and watch everyone else ride, and see what their problems are and how the clinician tries to solve them.

If the clinic is not in the area and you can't afford the auditing fee and a place to stay, offer to groom for someone who *can* afford it. For most clinic participants, a groom is well worth the expense of a few meals and half a hotel room (which the rider would have to pay for in any case). Anyone who has ever ridden in a clinic without any assistance will tell you that it is an indescribable relief to have someone around to groom the horse, roll bandages, walk the horse, take the horse away when the rider dismounts with shaking legs after an hour or two of intense concentration, poultice the horse, and so on.

At many clinics, each rider is allowed free auditing privileges for one groom—why shouldn't that groom be you? If nothing else, it will give you a chance to observe a number of clinicians and decide for yourself what you think of them and their methods. Grooming—especially if you become proficient at braiding manes and tails—can be made to pay, literally. You can take your skills to shows, either as someone's groom or as an itinerant braider. Braiding pays quite well. In fact, it can even let you take your own horse to a show; if you are willing to get up very early, you can braid enough horses to cover the cost of your own entry fees and trailering charges.

Some General Guidelines

Here are a few reminders for students who want to get the most from their lessons:

Be There If you have to cancel, do so well in advance of your lesson. Your instructor will be grateful for the notice, and you may save yourself some money—most instructors will expect to be paid the full lesson fee for a non-emergency no-show or last-minute cancellation.

Be on Time Late arrivals are usually flustered and hurried and insufficiently prepared. Don't waste lesson time on pre-lesson preparation.

Be Prepared When you enter the ring for your lesson, you and the horse should both be warmed up and stretched. The horse should be in good health and condition, and fit enough for the lesson—and so should you. If you aren't healthy or fit, let your instructor know so that she can modify her lesson plan accordingly.

Be Attentive You will get more from the lesson if you can put aside your other concerns and spend the time completely focused on your instructor, your horse, and your riding. Your progress will reflect your ability to concentrate.

No matter how much you know about horses and riding, you can always learn more. Lessons are the best investment you can make. If you and your instructor work together to increase your horse's abilities, then your own abilities, confidence, and knowledge will increase steadily until riding becomes a true pleasure for both you and your horse.

A Stable
Environment

You may find it odd that this chapter comes before the one on purchasing a horse. There is a reason: in this chapter, you will learn how to evaluate a boarding stable and how to arrive at a realistic estimate of your horsekeeping costs. Even if money is no object, finding the most suitable situation for your horse is not always an easy process—or a quick one. You need to find out what facilities are available in your area, what they will cost, and what will be best for your horse and most convenient for you, *before* you find yourself standing in the driveway with a leadrope in your hand, wishing you had known that Pretty Pony Farm had sold its cross-country course to developers, or that Happy Horse Stables had a six-month waiting list.

Much of the information in this chapter will be of use to riders who keep their horses at home, especially if they are considering leasing out their extra stalls to boarders. But for many riders, "keeping a horse" means keeping him at a facility owned and run by someone else. If your horse lives on your property, you have control over his quality of life. If you board your horse, his quality of life depends on the quality of the barn you select. Large commercial stables and small backyard barns both have their advantages and disadvantages. Whether your particular interest is dressage, eventing, or trail riding, you will want to find a facility that can accommodate you. You will probably have to make compromises—few facilities will meet *all* the criteria given here.

75

But whatever your riding style, you will need a stable that is safe, accessible, and affordable, and that offers appropriate instruction, or allows you to bring in your own instructor (more about this later). Every stable has benefits and drawbacks. This information will help you evaluate your choices.

Stable-Visiting

Before you visit a barn, you should call and talk to the owner, the barn manager, or the resident instructor. At most stables, someone will gladly show you around *by appointment*. On a tour, you can ask questions— what times do the horses get fed (useful information for working riders)? When do most boarders ride? Are lessons for boarders only, or do other people come in for lessons? Are shows held on the premises? On a tour, you can look closely at the feed, at the manure pile, inside the tackroom, the office, the lounge—places that you might not feel free to inspect on your own.

Visit on the days and at the times that you expect to do most of your riding. Ask about the arena schedule, the instructor's lesson schedule, and typical traffic patterns. Don't look at a large, damp, empty arena on Thursday night and think "Oh, lovely, I'll be very happy schooling in here," and then find out, after moving in, that the arena is always dusty and crowded on *your* riding nights: Monday, Wednesday, and Friday.

Your Inspection Tour

You can tell a lot about a facility before you ever step into the barn. Look at the land, the buildings, and the fences. Newness and fresh paint are attractive, but look more closely at what matters: solidity, cleanliness, and safety.

The driveway and parking area should be in good repair. The property should be tidy, and the buildings solid and safe, not crumbling or sagging. Fences don't have to be six feet tall or shining white, but they must be safe. There are many horse-safe fences: pole corral fencing, board fencing, v-mesh and diamond-mesh wire, and post-and-rail. A top strand of electric fence wire discourages horses from leaning over the

Janet Colby, 42, teaching assistant, with her
Lippizaner mare Patina ("Suzanne").

"Being a responsible horse owner takes a lot of work, thought, and planning.
Many of us aren't aware of how much it takes until we are in the situation.
Then we don't always know what our choices are. . . . We must board at a
facility where the management philosophy is as close to our own as we can
find. This will make it possible for the horse to have consistent care whether
we're home or away."

Two forms of horse-safe fencing.

fence. Barbed wire is unacceptably dangerous. Horses and barbed wire should not be on the same piece of land. Piles of old machinery—the junkyard look—is another danger sign.

Barns

Barns should be solid but never airtight; they must be well-ventilated. Some barns have no holes, no cracks, no gaps—and no air circulation. Heated barns can provoke respiratory disease in horses.

Flooring

Brushed or corrugated concrete flooring is easy to clean and doesn't cause horses to slip and slide. Dirt aisles don't cause slipping either but are harder to keep clean and tend to become uneven. Rubber matting over dirt or concrete flooring reduces noise and slipping, and provides a flat but cushioned surface.

Outdoor horses require shade and shelter.

A wide, well-lit aisle with sliding stall doors.

Aisles

Aisles should be clean, and all cleaning implements (brooms, rakes, pitchforks, skeps, and so on) hung or stored out of the way. Center aisles should allow horses to turn around easily. Since aisles serve as grooming areas and places for veterinarians and farriers to work, they should be well-lighted and equipped with crossties. Saddle racks should fold out of the way when not in use. A horse turning around in a narrow aisle, or being led past another horse in a wider aisle, can get caught on a fixed, protruding saddle rack.

Read the Signs

Some signs should be posted at every stable. "No smoking" is one—and it should be enforced with *no* exceptions. "No dogs" or "Dogs allowed on leash only" is another useful sign, both for the horses' and riders' sakes, and for the safety of the dogs. The barn rules should be posted, as should any warning signs. If signs are posted but you find empty first-aid boxes, useless fire extinguishers, people smoking, and loose dogs running about, then the signs are only a token concession to the idea of safety. And although it should go without saying, avoid barns where alcohol is a featured beverage. Whether it's the boarders, the staff, or the owners who drink, it's a red-alert danger to your horse. Like tobacco and drugs, alcohol has no place around horses.

Lighting

In addition to aisle lights, there should be stall lights: either a single bank of lights with a central switch to light all stalls on one side of the aisle, or individual stall switches. In either case, bulbs and wiring should be inaccessible to horses.

Stalls

Stall doors should slide along the wall or open outward, never inward. Each stall should have a card on it listing the horse's name, feed schedule, owner's name and phone, veterinarian's name and phone, and any special instructions. Stall size is important: unless your horse is very small, his stall should measure 10 × 12 or larger. Horses need room to turn around, walk around, lie down, and get up again without getting cast. Stall walls should be solid, with no gaps between the boards. A kicking horse can bend boards outward and catch a foot in a space that seems far too narrow to be dangerous. Each stall should have adequate ventilation. There should be no sharp edges, broken boards, protruding nails, or bare lightbulbs.

Stall Floors

Like aisle floors, stall floors can be dirt, or rubber mats over dirt or concrete. If the floors are dirt, check to see that they are kept reasonably level and that holes are filled in regularly. Rubber mats make good stall flooring if there is sufficient bedding on top of the mats. Over cement flooring, the mats will lessen the stress on the horses' legs. Over dirt flooring, they will keep horses from digging holes and creating an uneven surface.

Cleanliness of Stalls

Stalls should be clean and thickly bedded. Even just before stall-cleaning time, you should see clean bedding with a few piles here and there. You should not be overwhelmed by a strong ammonia smell. A clean, well-kept stable will smell of fresh air and horses, not of manure and ammonia. Ask about stall cleaning. If the stable staff does it, how often is it done? If the horse's owner elects to do it and then does not do it, will staff do it and charge the owner? This can be important if the neglectful owner's horse is stabled next to yours. Look at the manure pile. Is it small, tidy, and not too close to the barn or the horses? If so, it is a good, managed manure pile even if it isn't perfectly squared off. Or is it huge, messy, and crawling toward the barn? An out-of-control manure pile is not just an aesthetic problem; it is a smelly, disease- and fly-breeding fire hazard.

Water

Horses should always have fresh, cool, clean water. Water buckets should be clean and full. An individual horse may have drained his bucket, but if you look through the barn, most buckets should be full. If automatic waterers are used, the water in them should be clean and free from algae.

Feeding Program

Ask about the feeding program, and look at the feed. Feed should include hay, grain, and salt. Horses should be fed at least twice a day. Feed should be stored in covered containers, free from mold, mice, and dust, and the feedroom should be inaccessible to horses. Check the grain and hay: they should smell fresh and be easy to squeeze in your hand. If the grain is full of chaff or the hay is full of dry stems, it will be painful to your hand—and to your horse's mouth. There should be a feeding schedule posted, with each horse's name matched with feed amounts and special instructions.

Stable Neighbors

Look at the other horses at the barn. Do they look healthy, cheerful, interested in you? If they are all too thin, too fat, or if they turn their backs when you come in, think again. Well-treated horses are cheerful and curious; they will come to see who you are and what you are doing.

Turnout

Look closely at the turnout and pasture areas. Check the fencing, the gates, the water tank or creek, and the size and orientation of the shelter. Footing should be adequate and safe. It probably won't look like a golf course, and it may look like an unplanted field, but it should not look like a landfill site. The shed should not be knee-deep in manure. Find out how many horses use the area each day, how many are turned out at one time, and what the specific arrangements would be for your horse.

If the turnout area is a pasture, or if you are leasing a field, ask what is growing there. Check for poisonous plants—some plants and trees are toxic to horses. If you are unable to identify certain plants, you can take samples to your Cooperative Extension Service office for identification.

Good lighting and rubber mats make the farrier's task easier and safer.

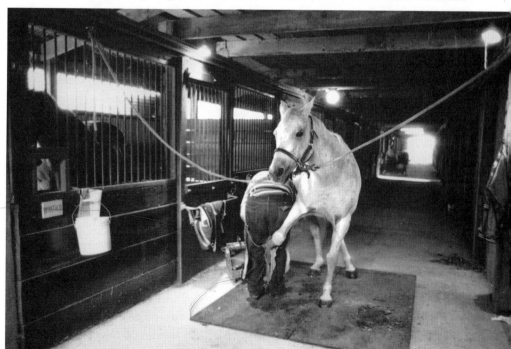

Look for a facility that can accommodate
your riding interests.

Riding Arena

Evaluate the riding arena in terms of safety, then in terms of the work
you want to do. Can it be closed off? Is it big enough for several riders
to use at once? If there are jumps in it, are they always there? This is
useful information, whether your main interest is jumping or dressage.
The arena surface should be firm, level, and flat, not uneven, pitted,
or rutted. The surface should be leveled, and the track filled in, regularly. It should also be raked or harrowed daily with light traffic, and
several times a day if traffic is heavy, as it would be at a busy
lesson barn or boarding stable. Arenas should be watered regularly to
keep the dust down, and should be kept picked clean of manure.
Dust from dried manure can create serious respiratory problems for
horses and humans.

Boarders should have someplace to keep their tack.

Tack Room

There should be a place for riders and boarders to keep their equipment: a tack room with saddle racks, lockers, or both. Find out whether the tack room is kept open or locked.

Toilet

Toilet facilities of some kind are essential, whether a heated, designated room or a portable toilet near the barn.

Lounge

A lounge is a wonderful convenience, especially if it is heated and equipped with a coffee machine. But the single most important item in the lounge is the *telephone*—a convenience for daily communication, and a lifeline in an emergency.

Preparation for Emergencies

Emergency Telephone List Every stable needs an up-to-date list of useful numbers posted near the telephone. The list should include the telephone numbers of local hospitals, ambulance services, cardiac rescue units, and other emergency services. It should also include the telephone numbers of local equine veterinarians and of the local veterinary hospital, if one is nearby. Prominently displayed somewhere—in red, or in a box marked "you are here"—should be the name, address, and phone number of the stable, together with simple directions from main roads. This information can be surprisingly hard to find during an emergency.

First Aid Boxes   Every stable should have two first-aid boxes: one for horses and one for humans. Both should be kept stocked and in an obvious place—in or near the tack room or the office, for instance.

Check to see that they are filled and accessible; a first-aid kit that is empty or locked won't be much help to anyone. If there is no first-aid box, make one. If you keep your horse at home or in a rented field, you will need to make your own first-aid boxes, stock them well, and keep them handy.

In Case of Fire   Every stable should have more than one exit. Every stable should have working fire extinguishers, and there should be a map posted showing the locations of all fire extinguishers and exits.

Instruction Options

Board Includes Lessons   Some teaching barns include lessons in the price of the board. Your monthly bill covers weekly lessons with the resident instructor, and the amount is payable whether or not you take those lessons. This can be a good arrangement *if* you want to take lessons with that instructor anyway. But there can be drawbacks to this arrangement. You may not be permitted to bring in another instructor, and if you don't get on with the resident instructor, you will be paying for lessons you don't take. Then, if you want lessons from someone else, you will have to go out of your way—literally—for the lessons you *do* want.

Bring Your Own Instructor   Most stables have a resident instructor or a regular visiting instructor. If you take lessons with someone else, be sure that there will be no problem if your instructor comes in on a freelance basis. It is unpleasant and frustrating to settle in at a barn and then find that your instructor isn't allowed to give you lessons there.

Lesson Stable   If the primary focus of the stable is a lesson program, look at the school horses. They don't have to be equine beauty contest winners, but they should be healthy, sound, fit, and friendly. Their tack doesn't have to be stylish, but it should be simple, well-fitting, and in good condition. Clean leather should be soft and shining; beware of stiff, cracked, dry, dirty leather on saddles and bridles. Bits and saddle pads should be clean. Even if saddles are shared, each horse should have his own bridle, saddle pads, and brushes.

The Ins and Outs of Horsekeeping

Some stables can offer several alternative arrangements for your horse: stalls, pasture, turnout, or some combination of these. You will need to evaluate each option in terms of your horse's needs and your own convenience.

Indoors

Many horses spend most of their lives in stalls. This is convenient for the owner but not for the horse. A stall is an artificial environment, and a horse living in a stall suffers from lack of room in which to exercise, lack of companionship, and boredom. A stalled horse needs a good deal of organized exercise each day just to maintain a reasonable level of fitness. A stalled horse is a confined horse and may develop the compulsive behaviors of confined horses: cribbing, weaving, and kicking. The sour horse is almost always an indoor horse. There are diseases of the indoor horse, as well; most cases of colic, thrush, and almost all respiratory infections occur in stabled horses.

Stalls are convenient for the owner. A horse in a stall can be clipped and blanketed, making it easier for the owner to cool out the horse effectively in winter. A horse in a stall is easy to find and halter—the owner won't have to walk across a muddy field and coax the horse to allow himself to be caught. A horse in a stall takes less time to groom. If you ride every day, or pay to have your horse exercised when you can't ride, the stall option may work best for you.

Outdoors

If you can keep your horse outdoors under suitable (safe, appropriate) conditions, do so. If your horse can live in a field of at least two to four acres, properly fenced, with a shelter from wind and rain, and with another horse for company, you will be doing the maximum to ensure his physical, mental, and emotional health.

An outdoor horse has certain requirements: safe fencing, safe footing, shelter, food, water, and access to salt. He also needs companionship, and enough space to provide room for exercise. Outdoor life is not maintenance-free. Water should be available to outdoor horses at all times, and their water tanks should be cleaned regularly. Manure must be removed from shelters on a weekly basis, if not on a daily one; in the field, manure will need to be picked up or harrowed regularly. Horses need companionship, but if the turnout area is only two or three acres, try to keep no more than two horses there. Overcrowded conditions often produce injuries. Horses that share living quarters need to be friends; be careful when adding to the group.

An outdoor horse can live happily without building up excess energy, even if he is ridden only two or three times a week. His freedom of movement allows him to use his energy in the way horses were designed to use it—by the constant gentle exercise of day-and-night walking around.

The outdoor horse, if unridden, will not maintain special-purpose muscles developed by specific work—upper-level dressage, say, or jumping. But he will maintain his level of fitness better than will a horse that lives in a stall, even if the stalled horse is ridden daily. Older horses living outdoors will be noticeably less stiff than their indoor counterparts. Horses need to keep their muscles toned and stretched; the time they spend walking in their field will do precisely that. The outdoor horse will provide you with more pleasant and predictable rides when you come out. And—no small thing for a working horse owner—this arrangement provides a benefit to you, as well: freedom from guilt if you aren't able to exercise your horse daily.

In-and-Out

Managed turnout is a reasonable compromise between what is convenient for the rider and what is best for the horse. Your horse will spend the evening and night in his stall. But during the daytime, he will be turned out for four or five hours. This benefits you because your horse is dry and accessible when you are most likely to have the time to ride. It benefits your horse because he has a daily opportunity to move about freely, relax, and socialize. Managed turnout can free you from the worry

A well-equipped office/lounge area.

and guilt that all right-thinking horse owners feel when health, weather, or circumstances at work or at home keep them away from the barn. You may miss a day or two of riding, but you will know that your horse's requirements for exercise and companionship have been met.

Schedule of Fees

At each stable, ask to see the schedule of fees for various types of board (stall, stall with turnout, pasture, and so on) and for types and amounts of feed. Some stables feed according to the horse's actual needs; others provide a set amount of feed (which varies from stable to stable) for one basic price; if your horse needs more feed, you will be charged more. Some stables provide salt, some expect you to provide it. There may be a fee for adding your supplements to your horse's feed. Your bill will generally include separate charges for any additional services. These might include stall cleaning, turnout, grooming, handwalking, longeing, putting on and taking off blankets or boots, applying fly spray, administering medications, holding the horse for the vet or the farrier—anything requiring extra time and effort on the part of the stable staff.

Comparing Costs

You will naturally rule out stables that charge more than you can afford, but visit them in person and get *all* the information before comparing costs. This is why you need detailed fee schedules; telephoning all the local stables and asking the price of a month's board will not get you the information you need to make a good decision. The price of basic board is often just a starting point; a seemingly less expensive stable may have hidden costs. Charges for extra hay and turnout for horse owners, or arena rental and lesson-horse surcharges for non-owners, can make the actual cost comparable to the amount charged by a more overtly expensive facility. Example: Barn A and Barn B are both within ten miles of your home. They have similar facilities. At first glance, board clearly costs more at Barn A. But if your horse requires daily turnout or more hay, Barn A's board includes these things, whereas Barn B charges extra for them. The added charges make Barn B the more expensive place to board.

Location and Hours

Proximity to home is generally a plus—but be flexible. If a stable offers excellent instruction, trained school horses, and great facilities, you may be willing to spend a little more time getting there and back. Horse ownership makes demands on your time, regardless of the circumstances. A do-it-yourself facility ten minutes from home might be as time-consuming as a full-board arrangement forty minutes away. You must decide whether you prefer to spend your time mucking out or driving.

Some stables are closed to boarders or students at certain times. If you live nearby and your schedule is flexible, you may not mind. But if your schedule is demanding, you may be unhappy if your stable has fixed hours. Find out how many people ride there and what schedules they follow. A busy lesson stable with a popular instructor may have a perpetually crowded arena. You might prefer a smaller, quieter stable, with a low-key, no-pressure atmosphere.

Atmosphere

The atmosphere of a stable is important. If a stable is managed by competent and caring horsepeople, and the atmosphere of the barn is professional, efficient, and businesslike, the boarders will tend to behave accordingly. At a lesson barn, the atmosphere will often be determined by the instructor. Watch the riders: their behavior will reflect the influence of the instructor.

Barn Behavior and Stable Manners

Your chosen stable may have a long list of rules, a short list, or—if you arrange to keep your horse at someone's private facility—no posted rules at all. Whatever the situation, you should be aware that most barn rules are based on safety, manners, or both. Their aim is to reduce hazards and keep interactions predictable, safe, and simple. Most are sensible and obvious: if you make a mess, clean it up; if you break something, fix it; if you open something, close it. In the absence of specific rules, these suggestions should help you get along anywhere.

Behavior (Human)

There should be no running or shouting in the barn, or sudden movements in front of horses. There should be no loose dogs or unattended children.

Leading

Horses should be under control at all times, either under tack or wearing a halter and leadrope (with someone holding the leadrope). Anyone leading a horse should use both a halter and a leadrope.

Crossties

Never leave a horse alone on crossties. If someone needs to move a horse past your crosstied horse, undo one side, let the horse by, then hook it up again. It takes very little time, and it's an easy way to avoid a nasty accident.

Grooming

Use your own tools, and put them away when you have finished using them. If the grooming kit belongs to the stable, put it back where you got it. If you are grooming a lesson horse, be sure to use *his* brushes, not those assigned to some other horse. It's a matter of health as well as convenience.

Bathing

Clean out the wash stall after you use it. You don't have to scrub it down with disinfectant, but do dispose of the dirt and hair that will otherwise block the drain. Hang up or coil the hose so that it will be handy for the next person.

Arena Use

Entering and Leaving

When you enter or leave the arena, watch for horses being ridden, longed, or led; people on foot; and so forth. You will want to enter without causing a commotion or a collision. The people in the arena will appreciate it if you announce yourself; if they know that another horse is coming in, they can get out of the way.

Longeing

If you are alone, longeing your horse, allow him to work on the largest possible circle; it will be much better for his legs. If another person is longeing, and there is room for both of you to longe your horses on a 20-meter circle—good. If not, take turns. It is far better to handwalk your horse than to stress his legs by longeing him on a small circle. If a rider enters the arena, reduce the size of your circle so that there is room on the rail. If the rider is a beginner and has little or no control of the horse, be flexible. Put away the longeline, and ride your horse, or come back later.

Loose Horse!

You have probably witnessed "loose horse" scenarios: rider falls off, horse trots away; longe line is dropped, horse canters off; child drops leadrope, horse runs off. If you are new to riding or to horses, you have probably wondered what you ought to do.

It's simple. The person who sees the loose horse first—generally whoever was once at the other end of the reins, longe line, or leadrope—yells "loose horse," and *everybody stops.*

If you're riding, stop. If the loose horse is galloping happily around the arena and you're unsure of your horse's reaction, dismount and hold him. If you're longeing, stop, coil your longe line, and hold your horse. If you're walking through the arena, stop. Loose horses, even when they start off at a gallop, generally calm down quickly if no other horses join them and nobody chases them. If there is no action around them, most will trot around for a few moments and then begin looking for food.

If you aren't holding a horse, you can help catch the loose horse *if* the owner or handler asks you to. Horses are easier to catch if *one* person goes after them. Most horses love to play tag, and if two or more people start after a loose horse, a game of tag is generally the result. If you think that you know a better way to catch the horse, suggest it, but don't act on it until the owner agrees. There may be something you don't know about that horse—a tendency to whirl and kick when approached from behind, for instance.

Safety

At any stable, the single factor that matters most is safety: for the horses, for the riders, and for the equipment (in that order). Your horse's safety must supersede all other considerations. And because his safety will depend on the stable owner's or manager's commitment to safety, you should choose intelligent, caring, knowledgeable management over fancy facilities if you can't find a stable that provides both. If your only choices are between two inadequately maintained stables, keep looking until you find a safe home for your horse. At an unsafe facility, your horse will eventually get hurt, and you will pay for it with your money, your time, and the knowledge that you failed to protect your horse. Your horse will pay for it with pain. The vet bills incurred by keeping a horse in unsafe conditions can be staggering. After a year or so, the total may represent much more than the difference between the cost of board at that stable and board at a better-maintained stable. The time you take to inspect and compare now will save you time and money later. It may also save your horse's soundness—or his life.

Stable Standards for Health

Entrance Requirements

Are there requirements for horses coming in? There should be. If your horse isn't allowed on the property without a record of his vaccination and deworming schedule, plus a current negative Coggins, rejoice. This is one of the hallmarks of a professionally run facility. Your horse will be much safer at this barn than at another facility with no such requirements.

Ask whether the stable checks boarder records at intervals, to be sure that your horse is still current for vaccinations, deworming, and a Coggins test. Again, a "yes" means safety for your horse.

Health Maintenance

Ask about the stable policy on routine health care. Some stable managers prefer to have all horses vaccinated and dewormed on the same schedule, for maximum parasite control. If so, find out what that schedule is. Ask what the procedures are if a horse is injured or becomes ill, and if the owner of an ill or injured horse is not available.

Insurance

Ask whether the stable carries insurance. Most stables require that boarders and students sign release forms, but liability insurance is not usually affected by release forms. If the stable has a liability insurance policy, ask to see it and make a note of the expiration date—this information is important.

Boarding Contracts

Some stables offer information packets to new boarders. Such packets generally include information about the facilities, a copy of the boarding contract, a list of barn rules, and a release-and-hold-harmless form for the boarder to sign and return.

Always have a boarding contract. Professionals will offer them as a matter of course. Contracts can be anywhere from one page to ten or more, but most of them will include:

- Your name, address, and telephone number(s)

- Someone to contact if you are unavailable

- Your horse's name and description (be as specific as possible: include markings, scars, brands, tattoo number).

- Your horse's feeding schedule and feed, including supplements

- Your veterinarian's name and telephone number

- Another veterinarian's name and number (in case your vet can't be reached)

- The boarding agreement itself. This should give detailed information about who is responsible for doing what with your horse, how often, and at what charge to you. It should specify who feeds and how often, who cleans stalls and how often, who provides salt, and so on. It might also specify who turns your horse out, where, with whom, how often, and for how long.

The boarding contract should list and describe everything that is included in the board, with specifics about *housing, feed, facilities,* and *hours.* It should also list the *schedule of fees,* the *methods of payment,* and *deadlines.* If your stable doesn't have a boarding contract, write your own. Cover all the bases you can before you get into an uncomfortable, confusing, or tragic situation.

Boarder Behavior

Here are some useful reminders:

- Pay your bill on time, every time. A boarding stable is a business.

- Be at the stable as often as you can. No matter how competent and dedicated the staff may be, unseen owners will not have the best-cared-for horses.

- Respect the staff—they are the people caring for your horse.

- Be considerate of others. Drive slowly, park carefully, clean up after yourself.

- Obey the barn rules.

- Don't assume anything that wasn't specifically laid out in the boarding contract, even if it "seems logical" or if it was included at your last barn.

- Know when to quit. Sometimes a boarding situation doesn't work out. But make the parting as calm and pleasant as possible. Circumstances change, stables change, owners change—and you might, someday, want to keep a horse there again.

Horsekeeping: the Bottom Line

If you are wondering whether you can afford to keep a horse, use the information you have acquired to calculate an approximate cost of horsekeeping. Don't figure in the cost of your lessons; those are a separate expense. They may cost slightly less if you have been paying a surcharge for the use of a school horse. But you will need to balance that difference, if any, against the need to purchase your own tack and grooming equipment.

To estimate your horsekeeping costs, begin with the amount that you would pay to keep a horse at the stable of your choice for one year (basic board plus additional charges). Figure your annual total for recurrent expenses such as deworming paste and shoeing (seven to eight times a year for each). Then add the annual cost of routine veterinary care and immunizations. You can even add the cost of a year's driving to and from the barn. The total will be the approximate amount you would need to support a horse for one year, assuming that the horse had no special requirements and remained healthy.

Divide by twelve to arrive at an approximate monthly figure. Now, open a savings account (be original, call it your "horse" account) and deposit this amount each month, as though you already owned a horse and were paying for his upkeep. This will serve two purposes. One is to show you whether what you want is realistic. The other is to put away money towards the purchase price of the horse, or to build a balance in your "horse" account against emergencies or special needs.

More Money than Time

If you have trouble finding the time to ride but can easily afford to keep a horse, arrange for complete-care board at the stable of your choice. In exchange for your money, your horse can be fed, watered, turned out, longed, schooled, groomed, poulticed, bandaged, braided, clipped, medicated, supplemented, held for the farrier and the vet, and even exercised on the hotwalker or the treadmill. All you will have to do is come out and ride.

Some Money, Some Time

If your money and time are about equally balanced, full board is probably your best option. For a fixed fee, the stable provides feed, stall, turnout, stall cleaning, and all bedding. Your responsibilities include providing supplements, grooming your horse, riding him, and cleaning your tack.

A less costly alternative would be partial or limited board. With this arrangement, the stable provides a stall, bedding, and feed. You are responsible for horse care, supplements, grooming, tack-cleaning—and for cleaning your horse's stall, turning him out, and bringing him back in again.

More Time than Money

An even more economical arrangement is stall rent. When you rent a stall, you get just that—a stall (sometimes you also get access to turnout or pasture). This resembles the partial board arrangement, but you provide the bedding and feed.

Another possibility is pasture board. This will include hay, water, and a shelter, but you will have to supply your own salt block and grain, and probably do your own feeding as well. The pasture will probably be unsupervised; you will be responsible for monitoring your horse's condition and health. Your horse, however, will be glad to be outdoors all day with company, living a relatively natural life.

Barter and Labor

At a small stable, you may be able to customize a do-it-yourself arrangement. At any stable, it may be possible for you to barter your services for board—it doesn't hurt to ask. If you have the time and the physical capacity, offer to work off some or all of your horse's board by feeding, watering, cleaning stalls, fixing or painting fences, exercising other horses, mowing pastures, or anything else on the list of chores.

If time constraints or physical limitations won't allow you to offer yourself as stable help, consider bartering your personal or professional skills instead. Do you have accounting experience? Offer to help keep accounts or do bookkeeping for the farm owner. Are you a graphic artist? Perhaps the owner would like to have a brochure designed for the farm.

Starting Over: Changing Barns

The time may come when you wish to leave your boarding barn and take your horse elsewhere. Even if you are very unhappy at the barn, try to make the break in a quiet, tactful way. Be reasonable about the things you dislike at the barn. No barn will be absolutely perfect or precisely to your tastes. Before you move, be certain that (a) you can't live with what you have now and (b) things really are better where you are going.

If you are determined to leave, check your boarding contract. Find out whether you are expected to give a month's written notice or whether a verbal "I'll be moving Prince next Saturday" will do. Most barn owners will be cooperative; many have waiting lists, and if you want to leave in a week instead of a month, they may be able to accommodate you. If no accommodation can be reached, the managers of your new barn will have to be patient. They will. After all, once you are there you will be expected to respect the terms of *their* boarding contract.

Before you leave, and after you leave, try not to criticize the barn or its owners. If someone asks why you left, you can always say, "It wasn't working out." You don't have to give details.

No Way Out

Sometimes your present barn, although horrible, is the only option you have—if you are waiting to get to the top of another barn's waiting list, for instance. In the meantime, don't despair even if you have been unable to improve your horse's situation through formal channels. With planning, cooperation, and a little time and money, you can improve your horse's living conditions and increase your peace of mind.

If the feed is poor-quality or inadequate, buy a large plastic trash can with a secure lid, and keep a supply of good-quality feed for your horse. If the barn hay is poor, think of it as roughage, and plan your horse's diet accordingly. If bedding is the problem, you may be able to buy extra or bring in your own.

If you worry that your horse isn't getting his supplements, take charge. Hang a container on his stall, and instead of loose supplement and a scoop, put in seven smaller containers marked with the days of the week.

Make friends with the other boarders; they probably share your concerns. But don't turn your common cause into a gripe session— be constructive. You can organize the boarding-stable equivalent of a Neighborhood Watch and check on one another's horses on a regular timetable.

Make the best of what you have until you can find a new home for your horse. And when you inspect that new barn, use your knowledge and experience to evaluate it from your horse's point of view. Where your horse is kept will determine, to a great extent, how healthy and happy he will be.

Successful Horse Hunting

When you begin looking for a horse, ask yourself why you want to be involved with horses; what sort of riding you most enjoy; and how much riding you will be able to do, how often, and at what level of intensity. Which horse is right for you? You will find the correct answer more easily if you are aware of your motivations, your goals, your level of fitness, and your professional, social, and financial realities.

When you shop for a car, you either (a) know enough to be an intelligent shopper or (b) bring someone else along to be intelligent on your behalf. You should take the same approach to horse-shopping. Even if you can judge looks, basic conformation, and temperament, are you equally confident of your ability to evaluate condition? movement? level of training? And are you ready to pronounce on a horse's health and soundness? For every inexperienced, first-time buyer who is lucky enough to stumble onto the horse find of the century, there are hundreds more who end up with totally unsuitable horses.

You may have fallen in love with a lesson horse, but good lesson horses are usually worth their weight in gold and are rarely available for purchase. The exception might be a lesson horse that can no longer stand up to the work, but is this a horse that is likely to satisfy your needs?

Leasing a Horse

Leasing a horse can be a good plan for a rider who isn't certain that she wants the full responsibility of ownership. A *lease* allows you to take on some or all of an owner's responsibilities without making a long-term commitment.

A *part-lease* is often convenient for a rider who lacks the necessary time and/or money to take on a full-time obligation. By part-leasing a horse, you can ride the same horse consistently, something that is not always possible when you ride lesson horses. The responsibilities of ownership and horse care are shared. A part-lease arrangement can also make it possible for two people to lease a horse together, or for one person to part-lease a horse belonging to the other.

The key to this arrangement is compatibility. The two people must have more in common than their desire to part-lease a horse. They must be compatible in other areas as well: riding ability, riding style, training goals, training techniques, and level of competence. They will also need compatible schedules: no matter how well two riders agree, the arrangement will not work if both ride only on weekends.

A *full lease* carries with it most of the responsibilities of horse ownership but not all its rights and privileges. To protect the horse and his owner, leasing contracts generally specify what the horse may be used for, where he may be kept, what regular veterinary and farrier care he will receive, and so forth. Details are important. The more things that are specified and spelled out in the lease agreement, the fewer surprises there will be. Whatever is not clearly understood *and put in writing* can be misunderstood. The subject of horse-care, for example, can become unpleasant if the horse's owner and the lessee disagree on, for instance, what constitutes a "regular" schedule.

One person may feel that the horse's feet should be trimmed and his shoes reset or replaced every four weeks; the other may feel satisfied if the farrier visits three times a year and trims the horse "whether he needs it or not." Feeding, shoeing, and the frequency of routine vet care all need to be spelled out. Never assume anything. Disagreements may be unpleasant for the owner and the lessee, but they can be catastrophic for the horse's health. If you lease a horse and are in doubt about something, call the horse's owner. Don't change *anything* without checking: medicine, a supplement, a saddle pad, a brand of fly spray, or the length of the horse's bridle path.

Sometimes it is possible to arrange a *lease with option to buy.* In many ways this is the ideal way to purchase a horse; it allows you to get to know the horse, and effectively have him "on trial" for much longer than most potential sellers would ever permit.

Which Horse Is for You?

The Free Horse

The free horse is rarely free. In fact, the free horse can be very expensive, unless you already own a large farm and win a young, sound horse in a contest. If a horse is being given away, there is probably a good reason for it. A horse may cost you nothing to acquire, but the hidden expenses of keeping him may put a permanent dent in your finances. Some horses have medical conditions that require constant special treatment, usually expensive. Others have chronic foot or leg problems, again requiring constant treatment, again usually expensive.

There are many good-looking, unsound horses available for the asking because their owners can't bear to have them put down and instead would prefer that someone else take on their problems. An advertisement for a free horse that "would make a good companion animal" is not referring to a sound, lonely horse that needs a job and a friend. It describes a horse that *cannot* be ridden and whose owner would prefer to send him to live in someone else's field, at someone else's expense.

Old horsemen used to say that it cost just as much to keep a bad horse as a good one. When horses lived on the range when they weren't working, and in a corral when they were, this may have been true. But it isn't true anymore. These days, it often costs *more* to keep a bad horse. If one horse costs twice as much as another, but both live for ten years after purchase and the "cheaper" one costs twice as much to keep—or costs no more to keep but can't be ridden—then which horse costs more?

The Black Stallion Syndrome

Taming the wild horse is a popular fantasy. Many adults go horse-shopping with a rearing, mane-tossing silhouette imprinted in their minds. You *can* have a wild horse if you want one: You can adopt a mustang from the Bureau of Land Management. If you have years of experience with horses, and are a competent and understanding trainer—or if you are humble and willing to learn, and have a resident instructor who is a kind and experienced trainer—then perhaps adopting a genuine wild horse would be a reasonable idea for you. But a genuine wild horse is not the same as a domesticated and trained horse who—through abuse or bad handling—is uncontrollable. *The spoiled horse is a bad bet for anyone.*

The Black Beauty Syndrome

Another pitfall for the unwary buyer, especially the kindhearted, sentimental unwary buyer, is the temptation to rescue a pathetic horse. Wanting to save an animal from a bad life is a kind and worthwhile ambition. But buying something thin and pathetic at auction just so that it won't go to the killers is not necessarily the best way to do this.

Some horses have sustained permanent damage, external or internal, and will never be suitable for riding or even for adoption. And the pathetic starved horse, like the pathetic starved dog, can be deceptive. The weak, gentle rack of bones may be naturally docile—or he may have been starved into submission. Some horses have become savage through their experiences with humans, and are quiet only when they have barely enough energy to stand upright. Starvation, like blood loss, is an effective tranquilizer.

If you have the farm, the time, the experience, and a good veterinarian, you may be ready to take on such a project. But there are better ways to rescue a horse.

Animal Rescue Organizations

If you want to make a neglected horse's life better, you can make a contribution to an animal rescue organization such as the Hooved Animal Humane Society (HAHS).

Starving, injured, weakened animals require the sort of veterinary care that most of us simply cannot provide. A good animal rescue organization, like any other good charity, can make the best use of every dollar donated. Because of their facilities, their professional veterinary assistance, and their knowledge and expertise, these people can get more results for your money than you ever could.

If you still want to give a neglected or abused horse a wonderful home on your farm, do it through the rescue organization. During the rehabilitation period, the staff evaluate the animals' temperaments, their physical potential, and their suitability for adoption. Many of the animals may be adopted once their major medical problems have been resolved.

What to Look For in a Horse

When you are ready to buy a horse, keep in mind the following considerations:

Disposition and Attitude   A good disposition is your first requirement. Without it, even the most beautiful and talented horse in the world is useless. Whatever your riding ambitions, you want a horse that has certain qualities: honesty, generosity, and stability. Handsome is as handsome does.

Conformation and Soundness   Next, look for a sound horse with conformation that will help him stay sound and that is suitable for your riding style and ambitions.

Movement/Ability   Finally, consider talent. If you want to compete, movement will matter. But if you find a sound horse with a good disposition and good conformation, the quality of his movement can probably be improved through correct training.

Price   On any given day, a horse is worth what someone will pay for him. The price for the same horse may vary from month to month, or from season to season, depending on how badly the owner wishes or needs to sell.

If the owner has no indoor arena or doesn't ride in winter, the horse may cost less in November than he did in May. No sensible person will keep a horse through the winter just to sell him in the spring, if there is any chance of selling him immediately.

The appearance of a horse—height, color, and markings—can also affect the price. There is a saying that "a good horse is never a bad color," but tall horses, trendy colors, and symmetrical markings generally cost more. If you fall madly in love with a horse of a particularly splendid color—a gleaming palomino or an obsidian black, say—stand back, squint, and try to imagine him covered in mud from nose to tail. If

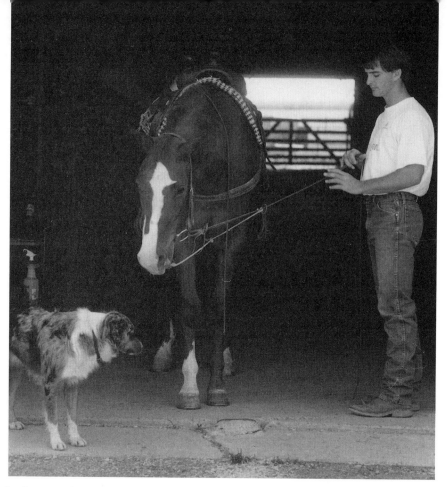

Suit the horse to the task.

his silhouette and way of going still leave you breathless, he may be the horse for you. But if he seems much less interesting without the color and shine, keep looking. Nowhere is the old adage "You get what you pay for" *less* true than with horses. Anyone shopping for a horse should remember that price and value are not the same.

Breeds and Suitability   You want a horse that can do what you want to do. The ex-jumper may never become a docile trail horse; neither may the old fourth-level dressage horse, that interprets each shift and nudge as a signal. Unless you have experience, time, and patience, it is a bad idea to buy something that has been bred and trained for one particular purpose and try to turn it to another. The most likely result is that both you and your horse will end up confused and upset.

Bloodlines matter if you intend to show in breed classes, or if you are purchasing a mare and plan to breed from her. Otherwise, your

Look for a horse that can do what you want to do.

gelding's bloodlines are much less important than his conformation, movement, and general demeanor. If you have a passion for a particular breed, do some research. Read books about the breed, watch videos, and talk to your instructor. Set yourself up for success, not for failure: reconcile your breed preferences with the sort of riding you want to do.

If you love Quarter Horses and are interested in pleasure or trail riding, or if you adore Arabians and want to do endurance riding, you will have many horses to choose from and will probably find exactly what you want. But if you want the exceptional Quarter Horse or Arabian that can go to the top in dressage competition, the odds are against you.

Don't begin with a dream of what you want to do and then buy something that isn't physically or temperamentally suited to the task. You'll make yourself miserable, and you'll make the horse miserable, too. If you acquire the horse first, take his physical and mental traits into consideration when you are deciding what to do with him. Most training successes (a happy, competent horse knowing what his job is and doing it well) are the result of someone looking at a specific horse, determining what he will probably do well, and training him accordingly. Match the task to the horse; don't arbitrarily decide that your horse must and will do something specific. If you want a magnificent, 17.3-hand, 1,800-pound Hanoverian, you and your horse will be better off if you want to do dressage, which he will probably do well, rather than endurance riding, which he might not survive.

What qualities do you most want in your horse? Are you looking for a spirited ride, a spectacular mover, or does your list begin with words like "sensible" and "good brakes"? If you are *not* competition-driven, you will have more options. There are any number of affordable horses whose fundamental soundness and pleasant attitude would suit you well. Any sane and sound horse should, with correct training, be able to do dressage up to Third Level (perform, that is, not necessarily win in competition) and jump fences up to 3' comfortably and safely. This is basic training for a good riding horse, just as the ability to ride a horse at Third Level dressage and jump fences to 3' means basic competence on the part of an educated rider. This is the starting point for professional specialization, but it is also a level to which we can all aspire. A single, independently wealthy rider might reach that level in just a couple of years. Someone with two children, a 9-to-5 job, and three riding days each week can expect to take a good bit longer to get to that point, but she can get there too if she is motivated and determined—and she won't need a "fancy" horse.

Beginning Your Horse Hunt

Hunt with a Camera

When you are horse hunting, take a notebook and a camera. If you like a horse, take notes—and photos. Get front, rear, and side views of the horse. Put the numbers of the shots somewhere in your notes (24 August, Oak Tree Farm, brown mare, shots 9–12). This will help you match your memories and your notes with the photos. If your camera puts the date on each photo, so much the better. Photos will keep your memory fresh and accurate (the bay gelding with the white foot—was he at the first or the third barn? Or—just a minute—maybe the bay *mare* was at the second barn; the bay gelding had *two* white feet, didn't he? Or was that the chestnut gelding?). Photos will also reveal details that may have escaped you at the time of your visit. The pictures might show, for instance, that the bay is built downhill, or that the gorgeous gray filly is tied in behind the knees.

Look at as many horses as you can. You will be able to eliminate most of them from consideration with no expenses other than your own time and transportation. Then, when you have cut your list of prospects down to two or three real possibilities, you can go back for a second visit. If possible, take your instructor with you to look at your semifinalists and help select the finalists.

Expect to pay for her time: this is a professional consultation. After the two of you have seen and ridden your prospects, and discussed them at length, you should know which of these horses is the one you would most like to own.

How to Look at a Horse

Look at the horse from all angles. See him walked and trotted towards you and away from you and from the side. If you still like him, then ask to see him ridden by his regular rider. Watch as he is tacked up. He should be quiet and cooperative, and his tack should be a simple bridle and saddle.

Watch as the rider mounts. Is the horse quiet? Does he stand until the rider signals him to move off? How does he move, and how does he react to being ridden? You want a cheerful, willing horse. If he goes badly for his regular rider, it's not a good sign. The horse should be alert and active; he shouldn't have been tranquilized or "worked down" for your visit. He should be willing and cooperative because he is trained, not because he is drugged or exhausted.

If you like the way the horse looks under his regular rider, have your instructor ride him indoors and outdoors at walk, trot, and canter; over water, over fences; through a dressage test—ask the horse to do everything he is supposed to know how to do. If she likes him, it's your turn. Ride quietly and carefully, and think about whether you like the feel of the horse.

The horse you buy should be the horse
you think you will enjoy most.

Consider whether his build suits your conformation. If you have short, heavy legs, don't buy a horse with a wide round barrel. You will feel as though you are sitting on a beer keg, and you will have little or no hope of learning to apply your aids correctly. A narrower horse will suit you better. If your legs are very long, the round-barreled horse may be just right. You will be able to sit comfortably and correctly without strain. You may also save money—a shorter horse with a wide barrel takes up as much leg as a tall narrow horse but may cost much less.

The horse you buy should be the horse you think you will enjoy the most. If you're pleased with the horse, his personality, and his way of going, and if your instructor thinks he is suitable for you, make an offer to purchase him if he passes his pre-purchase exam. The pre-purchase exam, depending on how detailed it is, is an up-front expense—but a worthwhile one. You can skip it, but please don't. And use your own vet or your instructor's vet. It is considered a conflict of interest for the seller's vet to do this exam.

The Pre-Purchase Exam

There is no such thing as a generic pre-purchase exam. Certain basic procedures will almost always be followed, but you and your vet will determine the number of procedures and how particular or exhaustive they are. Certain tests (X rays and special tests involving particular equipment) will be extra; you and your vet must decide which of these to do. When you first talk to the vet about doing a pre-purchase exam, find out what he charges and what his charges are based on (distance he has to travel? amount of time? number/type of tests? equipment needed?). Find out what sort of exam he will perform, what he will learn from it, and what sort of report he will give you. Discuss with him, *in advance*, any additional tests *and their costs*. He will then be able to plan to take enough time and equipment to perform all necessary tests, and you will know what those tests will cost.

Tell the vet about the horse he is going to examine: what he's done, where, with whom; how he's been trained; how he looked when you saw him ridden; how he felt when you rode him; and what your instructor said about him. The vet will need information from you, too. Be honest with your vet—and with yourself. Your vet will be looking at this horse in a particular context: what *you* intend to do with him. He can't evaluate the horse in a vacuum, and he isn't dealing with absolutes. Asking "How sound is this horse?" is like asking "How long is a piece of string?"

Your vet needs to know what kind of riding you intend to do and how much of it, and what sort of competitions you intend to ride in, how often, and at what level. He will need to know where the horse will be kept and how much daily exercise he will get. And if you are buying a mare and may want to breed her eventually, you should tell him that, too. Be as accurate as possible. If you say that you want a horse you can hack around the fields at a walk and trot, and then find—six months later—that your purchase doesn't stand up to the demands of jumping and galloping, you can't blame the horse, the seller, or the vet. If you have plans, goals, or ambitions, tell your veterinarian. That elderly retired eventer might be the perfect horse to teach you the basic skills of eventing; you could probably even compete him at the lower levels. But if you plan to compete all summer, every summer, and go up a level every year, the old campaigner may not be able to hold up.

General Health

This is the most basic, elementary, and inexpensive part of the physical exam. It will tell you whether the horse has anything overtly, grossly wrong with him—but it won't tell you a lot more than that. A general health exam is an overall check of the horse's body systems.

Your vet will probably begin by checking the horse's eyes and his TPR (temperature, pulse, respiration). He will check the horse's respiratory system: nostrils, sinuses, larynx, trachea, lungs. He will look at what's visible and listen for any unusual sounds that might indicate the presence of fluid or tissue which shouldn't be there.

He will listen to the horse's heart. Irregular beats could mean a congenital condition—possibly leaky valves. Heart murmurs are very common in horses; many are not a problem. If the horse has been raced, the vet will check his jugular veins. Some racehorses are given so many drugs by injection that these veins become scarred.

He will check the horse's digestive system by listening to gut sounds and looking at the horse's mouth to see whether the teeth and tongue are in good shape. He will also check to see whether the color of the gums and mucous membranes is normal.

The vet will check the horse's body for symmetry: his feet, legs, and muscles should be equally developed on both sides. He will examine the horse's body for sore areas, bony growths, damaged ligaments and tendons. He will also check for old scars. Like the tiny dents and seams in a rebuilt car, surgical scars from nerving or colic are often invisible, but they can be felt.

The vet will be looking for evidence of previous or current strain or injury, and for possible sites of future strain or injury. Evidence of a past injury won't necessarily eliminate the horse from your consideration.

"Soundness" means "soundness that affects performance," and an old splint which doesn't interfere with tendons or ligaments is only a cosmetic problem.

Any horse that has been worked for a few years is likely to have some "jewelry"; any horse of ten or older will probably show some arthritic changes on his X rays. Age and training level make a big difference: X rays that would be unsatisfactory in a two-year-old may be perfectly acceptable in a fourteen-year-old horse that is eventing sound without medication.

The vet will perform flexion tests, in which he will flex all the horse's joints and compare their responses. He will use hoof testers to check each hoof for abscesses, bruising, and navicular pain. If the horse is shod, he will look at the shoes: they may tell him something about the horse's soundness. If the horse is wearing pads, the vet will probably want to see the horse with the shoes and pads removed.

Conformation

The vet will evaluate the horse's conformation in terms of performance. The suitability of any horse's conformation will depend on what the horse does, and on what you want to do with him. A champion halter horse, for instance, might have tiny feet, straight hind legs, and a lot of extra weight. You could change his weight but not his feet or legs—this horse wouldn't be an ideal dressage or jumping prospect.

Movement

The vet is looking for soundness problems, not for quality of movement. A horse can be a short, choppy mover and still be sound. Finding the quality of movement you want is up to you and your instructor.

The vet will generally want to see the horse on the leadrope, on the longe line, and under saddle. He will ask to see the horse trotted towards him, then away from him, on a hard flat surface. This will tell him whether the horse's feet travel straight and whether there is any lameness present.

In veterinary hospitals and at international three-day events, vets inspect horses as they are trotted on a hard surface. If there is any question in your vet's mind about a possible lameness, he may ask to see the horse longed or ridden at a trot, in a circle, on a hard surface.

The spavin test consists of the vet flexing the horse's stifle and hock, holding them for two minutes, then watching as the horse is trotted away immediately. Any unevenness is bad, but stiffness may not be a problem, as long as the horse seems equally stiff in both hind legs.

On the Longe

The vet will probably ask to see the horse longed in both directions at walk, trot, and canter. This will bring out any front leg or inside hind leg problems. The vet will be looking for easy, rhythmic, regular movement and transitions.

Under Saddle

The vet will want to find out whether the horse has any problems in his back or in his hind legs. He will ask to see the horse ridden on a loose rein, at walk, trot, and canter. He will probably ask to see circle work—everything shows up on a circle.

He will then ask the rider to gallop the horse until he is breathing hard: this will bring out any respiratory problems such as roaring or heaves. If the horse is too young or unfit to be galloped, the vet can still test the horse's wind by having him breathe into a plastic bag. Respiration will be stressed as the oxygen is depleted, and the horse will breathe harder, just as if he had been galloped. If the horse *is* galloped, the vet can check the horse's pulse and respiration—stress rate and recovery rate—when the rider pulls up. This would be the end of most soundness exams.

Additional Tests

There are many other tests your vet can perform. Before he does them, though, you should ask him which tests he feels would be appropriate. You know what you can afford to pay; he knows what you need to find out.

Making Your Decision

Most horses have some problems; the question is whether you can live with a particular horse's problems or whether they will make him unsuitable for your purpose. You and your vet will have to use your judgment. Every "using" horse will have some wear and tear, and will have some irregularities eventually (you should see your own X rays!). Whether his performance will be affected, and to what degree, is another matter.

Many horses with questionable X rays are working sound, and some horses with clean X rays are unsound. If the seller has a set of old X rays that can be used as a baseline, you are in luck. If the lumps and bumps that appear on the new X rays are similar to the ones on the old X rays, and the horse has been sound, you probably shouldn't worry about the irregularities. But if the horse is young and the X rays from two years ago were *much* cleaner, then the vet will probably worry—and so should you.

What the Vet Can—and Can't—Tell You

The vet is conducting a medical exam, not an evaluation of the horse's athletic or competitive potential. He can't tell you whether this horse is talented, gifted, a potential big winner—whether your future competitive success is assured. He also can't tell you what the horse's value might be. What he *can* tell you is whether, on the day of the veterinary exam, this horse appeared to be physically able to do the things that you said you intended to do with him.

A pre-purchase exam is not graded pass/fail. Rather than saying "Yes, he can do it" or "No, he can't," your vet will perform the exam, tell you his findings, and help you interpret them. What you are asking for, paying for, and getting is a *professional opinion*. You and your instructor or trainer will be largely responsible for the horse's future performance; the vet can tell you only what the medical exam tells him about the horse *today*.

Your vet knows that what he sees when he looks at a horse on Tuesday morning is what he sees on Tuesday morning. And all he can tell you is what he sees then—not what he thinks or hopes he might see on Thursday or Friday or a month from now. And remember that, like doctors, veterinarians are aware of our national tendency to litigate. Because of this, they are becoming more hesitant to pass a horse as "sound," either generally or for your particular purpose.

Many people try to economize by skipping a pre-purchase exam on a horse that will cost them thousands each year to maintain. Many of those same people eventually pay for an equally expensive, but less useful, "post-purchase" exam to find out what is wrong with the horse they bought.

Know Yourself

Before you buy a horse, consider your immediate needs and your eventual goals. Know yourself. Will you be able to purchase a horse to ride or learn on now, and then sell him in a few years and buy something else? You are an adult—by now you should know what kind of person you are. If every animal that has ever entered your home or your life has stayed with you until it died of old age, you had better realize that the horse you buy will probably have a home for life.

If you can ride only on weekends, and want to lower your stress levels by having a pleasant day or two walking the trails, don't buy a high-powered show horse that expects and needs daily work. You won't be able to meet each other's needs. Your horse will be ready to explode under you when you finally saddle him; you, on the other hand, will probably be tired, frazzled, and in need of a quiet ride. If you plan to school your horse for an hour or more each day, six days a week, and compete on the weekends, you won't be happy with the pasture potato whose favorite gait is a slow walk. If you know your abilities, your ambitions, your goals, your schedule, and your financial capacity, and can communicate this information to your veterinarian, you will stand a very good chance of finding the right horse for you.

Economy Measures

The better-informed you are about horses and riding in general, about your chosen discipline in particular, and about the nature and purpose of a pre-purchase exam, the more money you can save. Save the pre-purchase exam for the horse you really want to buy, then use it to learn as much as you possibly can.

Arrange to have your vet check the horse for you on your third visit. This may cost a few hundred dollars—and it may save you thousands. When horse-hunting, we all have a tendency to choke on this particular expense, thinking "Oh, it'll cost so much, can I really afford to have a vet check this horse?" This is the wrong question. The right question is "Can I really afford *not* to have a vet check this horse?"

Get All the Information

In the last chapter, you learned how to figure your horsekeeping costs. Although horse expenses are not quite as predictable, or as constant, you can benefit from the same sort of cost-figuring. The initial purchase price is the least important of your horse-related expenses. Upkeep, on the other hand, is something you will continue to pay for as long as you own that horse. Some horses cost more to keep than others, and not just because they eat more (although that too can be a consideration).

Feeding

There is such a thing as a "hard keeper"—a horse that requires lots of feed. Some boarding stables feed according to horses' needs, but many boarding plans allow a certain amount of feed per horse as "basic board" and charge the owner for any extras. An extra two flakes of hay and four pounds of grain each day can add up. Over the course of a year, this horse will be noticeably more expensive to maintain.

Shoeing

Shoeing costs vary according to where you live and what sort of shoeing your horse requires. Special or corrective shoeing costs more than ordinary keg shoes. And steel shoes reset every six weeks are much cheaper than aluminum shoes with pads, reset every four weeks. A horse that needs any kind of shoes at all is going to cost a *lot* more over the course of a year than a horse that can simply have his feet trimmed. A horse that is comfortable, happy, and sound when barefoot is nice to own. Some horses hunt and show successfully with bare feet.

Supplements and Medications

If the horse is currently being fed seven different vitamin and mineral supplements, you can probably discontinue most of them. Your horse may thrive on hay, grain, water, salt, and *one* supplement that your veterinarian recommends. If your horse requires special medications or supplements, try to find other boarders at your stable that use the same supplements. If you can order the largest possible size of whatever it is, you will all pay less per unit.

Returning a Purchase

What happens if you bring your new horse home, only to find that he isn't what you thought he was? Even if you did everything right when you bought him—inspected him thoroughly, watched him ridden by his regular rider and your own instructor, rode him yourself, and asked your veterinarian to evaluate his soundness and suitability for your purposes—something may still be wrong. Your new purchase may be lame, unsuitable for the work you had in mind, or have a stable vice that wasn't mentioned by the seller or noticed by you. In a case like this, what can you do?

If there is something seriously wrong with your new horse, you may actually *have* some recourse. Horse sales, especially the casual handshake-and-check ones that often occur when you are buying a horse from a private individual, are not always permanent. You are a purchaser, the previous owner is a seller, and yes, you have some rights. The selling of horses is governed by a set of laws called the Uniform Commercial Code. These laws apply to any merchandise sold, *including horses*. The laws are not uniform from state to state, so you will have to find out the specifics for your state, but they are sufficiently similar that it is possible to provide some general information about them.

Under these laws, the important question is, Was the horse misrepresented by the seller? If so, in what specific way was he misrepresented? To be considered relevant, a misrepresentation must involve material facts. This means that the misrepresentation must have had a clear effect on the sale (you wouldn't have bought the horse if the claim hadn't been made) or on the price (you paid X amount because the horse was sold to you as a quiet, reliable field hunter, whereas in fact he becomes uncontrollable at the sight of hounds).

Do you have a contract? Sit down with it and compare it with the actual horse point by point. If the tattoo number doesn't match, or if the horse was sold to you as a child's mount but is a raving maniac, you may have a clear case for returning your purchase and getting your money back. If you have no contract, write down everything you can remember about the discussion(s) you had with the seller of the horse. If he said, "This horse can jump 4 feet," and the horse stumbles over a 2' crossrail, you may have a case. If, on the other hand, *you* said, "He looks like a jumper," and the seller said, "Um" or "Maybe so" or "Yeah, sure does," you don't have a case.

You can't return a horse because of a claim that the seller didn't make. If you just assumed that a horse must be sound because he looked so nice, or that he could jump because he was stabled at a jumper barn, you may be stuck with him. But if you asked specifically for a horse you could ride in "B" hunter shows, and after the horse is delivered you notice that he is blind in one eye (you should have paid for that pre-purchase exam . . .), that horse was misrepresented *by implication*. Once you had asked to see a show hunter, you should never have been shown that horse. In this case, you would have legal recourse.

Not all misrepresentations are deliberate, and not all of them require action. The exact age of a horse is sometimes unclear, even to a vet: Teeth may be misleading, depending on a horse's age and how he has been fed, and tattoos are notoriously difficult to read. If you bought a "ten-year-old" Thoroughbred gelding for your daughter, and she is delighted with his attitude and ability, does it really matter if his age is really fourteen?

More Money than Time

You can buy a horse trained to the level at which you want to ride, or want to learn to ride. Some successful, well-known dressage riders began this way, but it requires an enormous amount of money for the horse and for the lessons you will need.

Some Money, Some Time

You can purchase a lower-level horse trained within your chosen discipline, learn to ride him, and bring him on. This will be less expensive; the horse will cost less, and so will the lessons. As an alternative, consider an equine schoolteacher. Many highly successful competition horses reach an age at which their performance level drops and their soundness becomes questionable. Even though they can no longer compete at the highest levels, they can bring on riders who need to know what correct movement feels like.

More Time than Money

If you have the experience, the time, and the patience, you may choose to buy a promising young (unstarted) animal and bring him up. The challenge and the satisfaction can be immense, but the rewards won't be immediate, as they would be with an older horse. Still, a young prospect makes a wonderful second horse if your first horse is older, well-trained, and not very sound. An alternative would be for you to purchase a sound, older, lower-level horse and see whether you can take his training further.

Financial planning will help. Having to put off buying a horse because you don't have the money can be a frustrating experience, but it is nothing when compared to the frustration and desperation you will feel if you have to give up your horse because you find out too late that you really can't afford to keep him.

In chapter 6, you learned how to estimate the monthly expenses of horse ownership. In that chapter, I suggested that you open a separate savings account and deposit that sum of money into it every month while you prepare yourself for horse ownership and look for your ideal mount. This procedure will serve several purposes. For one thing, it will give you a realistic idea of the effect a horse will have on your disposable income. If you can't do without that money—and remember, that's just normal maintenance, no special vet bills, clinics, or competitions—then find out *before* you buy the horse.

What if, after a few months, you haven't found a horse yet but you are comfortable financially, managing fine without the money? That's a good sign. But keep depositing that sum in the account every month until you find your horse. When you *do* find him, that money can help you buy him or help pay for the pre-purchase exam. It might go towards a horse trailer, or a tack trunk full of lovely new tack. Or, if you are very sensible, it might stay in the account ("Horse Money," remember?) until you suddenly need something expensive—a chance to ride with a really wonderful clinician 200 miles away? a big trailer repair? a medical emergency—say colic surgery? Whether it's an opportunity that can't be missed or an emergency that can't be avoided, that money can help you deal with it.

Enjoying Your Horse

Whatever your horse is, whatever he looks like, you can work with him, you can improve him, and you can have a good time doing it. Although some breeds and types of horses are better suited to certain disciplines, as long as you and your horse both enjoy what you are doing, there is no reason not to go on doing it.

If you enjoy competitive dressage but worry that your horse is unsuitable for some reason—size? breed? color? movement?—ask yourself why dressage appeals to you. If what you really want is competitive success, then perhaps you would be happier with another horse.

But if what you enjoy is the process of making your horse the best horse he can be, then go right ahead and work with him. You won't turn a 14.2 Arabian into a 16.3 Dutch Warmblood—but so what? You can turn him into the very best 14.2 Arabian he could possibly be, and learn a lot about riding, training, and horsemanship in the process. Take that "unsuitable" horse as far as you can: make him the most athletic, the most fit, the most cooperative and happy horse in your area. Don't let anyone talk you out of a horse you love and enjoy; you may never find one quite like him again.

Equipment for Horse and Rider

Some riders are minimalists; others are tack junkies. Some people can pack one saddle, one bridle, and one halter and drive two hundred miles to a competition. Others—myself included—can't manage to attend a local schooling show without packing two saddles, two bridles, an extra pair of reins, spare stirrup leathers, an extra girth, a stable halter, a shipping halter, and an extra halter in case one breaks.

Your Starter Set

Your tack essentials will include a saddle, a bridle, a bit, reins, a girth, stirrup leathers, stirrups, and a saddle pad. Beyond these basic items, there is an infinite array of auxiliary equipment: martingales, breastplates, and so forth. New saddles are generally sold alone; your saddle pad, girth, leathers, and stirrups must be purchased separately. Bridles are sold without a bit, and frequently without reins. This allows you to customize your bridle, but it also means that your bridle will cost more than your first glance at a tack catalog would indicate.

Saddles

Saddles come in a wide range of styles and purposes. There are general-purpose and specialty Western saddles, including models designed

Cathy Capel, 39, owner/manager/instructor, Long Leap
Farm, and her Holsteiner gelding, Clemson.

"Don't make impulsive decisions on the purchase of horses,
tack, services, vehicles, etc. Research all but the smallest
purchases."

especially for reining, roping, and barrel-racing. There are Australian
stock saddles, saddle-seat saddles, endurance saddles, close-contact
show-jumping saddles, hunting saddles, eventing saddles, "all-purpose"
saddles, and dressage saddles.

Style   Select the style that suits the sort of riding you intend to do.
The saddle must fit the horse: this should be your first concern. It should
also fit you; if it doesn't, you will be uncomfortable and unable to ride at
your best. You will, in other words, be inconvenienced. If the saddle
doesn't fit your horse, it can cause pain and physical damage.

Cost Saddle prices vary widely according to the workmanship and the quality of the leather. You can easily find an inferior saddle for an elevated price, but you are unlikely to find a new, cheap, good-quality saddle. Get the best saddle you can buy for the amount you can afford to pay. A good saddle, new or used, is an investment in your riding.

Safety Once you have a good saddle that fits your horse well, maintain it properly. Equipment failures can cause accidents, and equipment generally fails because of neglect, misuse, or because the materials and the manufacturing were inferior. The most vulnerable parts of a saddle are those involved in attaching the girth. Saddle billets should be replaced when the holes stretch and the leather begins to crack between them.

You can't see how the billets attach to the saddle tree, which is a compelling reason to purchase a good-quality saddle. The billets of a well-made saddle are stitched to two pieces of webbing that pass either around or over the tree. (This is why girths should be fastened to the first and third billets, leaving the middle one for a spare; the first and second billets are attached to the same web.) The billets of many inexpensive saddles are attached insecurely and improperly to the saddle tree—sometimes with tacks! An abrupt stop, an enthusiastic buck, or a sudden shy can cause saddle and billets to part company.

Stirrup Leathers Stirrup leathers are made from a variety of leather types, all of which stretch to some degree. You will notice that they seem to face the wrong way. The finished, "grain" side faces inward because that side is tougher and more resistant to the wear caused by the eye of the stirrup iron. Unless your leathers are very new, don't rely on the numbered holes to tell you whether the leathers are the same length. Your stirrup leathers won't stretch to the same degree; the one on the left side will become longer, as it is subjected to extra strain when the rider mounts and dismounts. This won't be a problem if you switch the leathers each week so that each one spends an equal amount of time on the left side of the saddle.

Bits, Buckles, and Stirrups

Nickel is easily broken or bent: avoid it. A broken bit or stirrup, or a crushed stirrup, can put your life and your horse's at risk. Good stainless-steel bits and stirrups won't break or twist, and will last for many years.

When purchasing any metal bit, check it visually for bubbles and pits, then feel it carefully with your hands. If there is a sharp edge somewhere, find it before your horse does. Sharp edges can cut the edge of a horse's mouth. If you prefer loose-ring snaffles, check the holes where the rings pass through. Their edges can become thin and sharp with age.

Check your bits regularly; they can develop pits or sharp edges while they are in use. If your bit has a copper mouthpiece, check it daily. Copper is relatively soft, and teeth can create ridges in the mouthpiece or cause it to dent and distort. Teeth can also cause sharp ridges to form in rubber bits.

Be sure that the bit you buy actually fits your horse. Many riders buy bits by size only, without considering whether the shape of the bit suits their horse. Bit width (the width of your horse's mouth plus 1/2″) is a good starting point, but there are other things to consider.

Know Your Bits   If you understand the design and function of bits, you will make fewer mistakes in their purchase and use, and your horse will be more comfortable. A snaffle works by direct pressure: when you tighten the reins, the amount of pressure you feel in your hand is the amount of pressure the horse feels in his mouth. Snaffles can be straight, curved, or jointed (with one or two joints). They can be made of rubber, nylon, steel, copper, or alloy; they can be thick, thin, smooth, twisted, or have keys dangling from the center of the mouthpiece. They can have flat rings, D-rings, half cheeks, or full cheeks. They *all* work on the principle of direct pressure, and they put pressure on the bars, the tongue, and the corners of the horse's mouth.

A curb works by leverage: when you tighten the reins, the amount of pressure the horse feels in his mouth is greater than the amount of pressure you feel in your hand. A bit that works by leverage is a curb, no matter what the mouthpiece looks like. The length of the shanks determines the amount of leverage: the shortest shanks provide the least amount. When you tighten the reins, the shanks apply pressure to the poll, and the curb chain applies pressure to the horse's chin groove. If the bit has a port, the port applies pressure to the horse's tongue and to the roof of his mouth.

Know Your Horse's Mouth   A fat eggbutt snaffle is generally considered a kind bit, but it may be too thick—literally too much of a mouthful—for a horse with a small, short mouth or a thick tongue. Similarly, a horse with a low palate, a thick tongue, or both, may experience severe pain when the nutcracker effect of a jointed snaffle (thick or thin) causes the joint to dig into the roof of his mouth. This horse would be happier in a straight-bar or Mullen-mouth snaffle, or in a French-mouth snaffle, where the comfortable, two-joint construction leaves room for the horse's tongue. If your horse reacts badly to a smooth, well-fitting bit, have his teeth checked. They may have developed sharp edges that are rubbing or cutting his cheeks.

More Money than Time

If you have money but little time to shop for tack or clothing, you can patronize your local tack shop, and order from the major retail saddlery catalogs, which offer full descriptions and color photos of the items. You won't find many bargains, but you will shop with maximum information, speed, and convenience. In a hurry? You can order by telephone, charge purchases to a credit card, and have them sent by air express.

Some Money, Some Time

Mid-range shoppers should collect discount tack catalogs. The prices are definitely lower than in the major retail catalogs, but you will have to know more about the merchandise. Not all items are illustrated, and not all illustrations are accurate.

When reading any catalog, you must know how to interpret the information on the printed page. Catalog text can be deceptive. "English-style" is *not* the same as "English leather," which is *not* the same as "Made in England." Sound-alike brand names are common: some firms try to take advantage of the international reputation of a well-known saddlery by marketing their own, less-well-made items under a name that is similar enough to cause confusion, and dissimilar enough to avoid litigation. There are other forms of association: a "Stübben-style" saddle is *not* a Stübben saddle; a "Hermès-style" saddle is *not* a Hermès. Become familiar with good-quality saddlery so that you can use catalogs to your best advantage. Your knowledge will help you to sort out the facts, the hype, and the mistakes.

If a catalog description doesn't mention something that matters to you, consider writing or phoning the company to find out what you need to know. As a rule (this is true for mail-order purchases generally, not just for saddlery and tack), relevant, attractive *facts* that make good selling points aren't accidentally left out of advertising or catalog copy. If a saddle is made in Germany or England, this information will be prominently displayed. If a saddle is made in Japan, Argentina, or India, the country of origin may not be mentioned.

Bridles

Never compromise on your bit or reins, which affect your safety. The bridle itself is less important, as long it is comfortable for the horse. The function of the bridle, after all, is to keep the bit in place in the horse's mouth; a good bit held on by a well-fitting bridle made from braided string would be perfectly functional for everything except showing.

Style   When it comes to style, be conservative, especially if your budget will allow you to purchase only one bridle. A simple bridle made of good-quality leather, flat or raised, will always be acceptable in the show ring. Trendy tack—round, braided, studded with metal, or lined with colored leather or plastic—can be expensive because of its initial cost and because you may have to replace it when the next tack fad comes along.

Browband   Be sure that the browband fits easily and comfortably across your horse's forehead, neither sagging loosely nor rubbing his ears. If it is too small, it will be uncomfortable.

Reins

Reins can be plain, laced, braided, rubber-covered, rubber-lined, web, with or without leather stops. Your choice will be dictated by your style of riding, your personal preferences, and—if you show—by the requirements of the show ring. Buy good quality, and pay particular attention to the part of the reins that curves around the bit. This is where most of the wear and tear happens, and this is where you are most likely to find cracks in a pair of inexpensive or used reins.

Reins should be wide enough for you to hold comfortably. Most adults and many older children prefer a 3/4" rein; larger adults often favor a 1" rein. Even an adult with small hands should try to find reins that are at least 5/8" wide. Very narrow reins suit tiny children, but adult hands hold narrow reins by making tight fists, which cause tension all through the rider's arms and upper body. Riders with arthritic joints

Simple, plain tack is never out of style.

will find that a wider, thicker rein can be held securely with less effort. Rubber-covered reins can be especially comfortable for weak or stiff hands.

Saddle Fittings

Buy good-quality stirrups, leathers, and girths. Solid, stainless-steel stirrups and girth buckles (never buy chrome-plated *anything*) are an investment in your personal safety. So are leathers and girths made from good-quality leather. Fit also affects safety: cheaper stirrups that offer 1/2″ clearance on either side of your boot are preferable to expensive ones that are too small. Rubber stirrup pads are inexpensive, and give your boots some cushioning and added grip.

Pads   Saddle pads offer the rider great opportunities for self-expression. Color, fabric, trim, piping, monograms, pockets, special "shock-reducing" inserts—your choices are virtually unlimited. Of course, you also have the opportunity to save money by ignoring all tempting and expensive options. The essential purpose of a saddle pad is to keep the underside of the saddle clean.

Saddle construction and stuffing, *not the pad or pads*, determine saddle fit. If your saddle doesn't fit your horse, stuffing the space between them with a hard foam pad, a fluffy fleece pad, and a "bump" pad may make you feel better, but it doesn't make the saddle fit better and it can make the horse feel worse. Pads can be a short-term help, but they are not a long-term solution to the problem of a saddle that just doesn't fit.

The saddle must fit the rider, too. When a saddle forces a rider to sit too far back, the rider will often use a "bump" pad to lift the rear of the saddle. But as the back of the saddle comes up, the pommel is forced closer to the horse and can cause the tree to dig into the horse's withers or shoulders.

Your saddle should fit your horse—and *you*. Even expert riders find it virtually impossible to achieve a correct position in a badly designed or badly fitting saddle.

Used Tack

If you want affordable, good-quality tack, consider purchasing used items. Unless you are very knowledgeable about saddlery, you should avoid auctions. But you *can* find good used tack outside of tack shops.

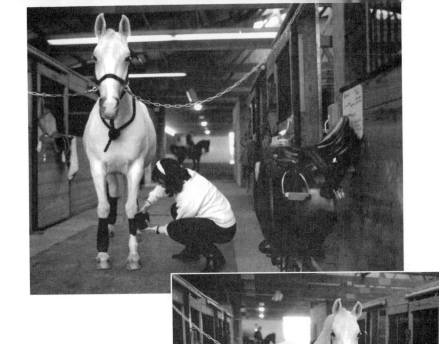

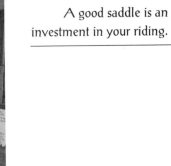

A good saddle is an investment in your riding.

Good saddles and bridles are often sold for low prices by people who haven't actually priced saddles since they bought theirs ten or fifteen years ago. You can get genuine bargains from private individuals who will be delighted to sell their saddles for what they paid for them new. And you will be delighted too, as prices may have doubled, tripled, or even quadrupled since then.

Good-quality, properly conditioned, properly looked after tack should last a long time. Saddles were once expected to last a lifetime; even now, a good saddle properly cared for should last fifty years and more. If your budget is limited, buying second-hand tack can allow you to own equipment that you couldn't possibly afford to buy new.

Finding Used Tack

Here are some suggestions for locating used tack:

- Visit local tack shops. They may have used saddles for sale, either on consignment or because they accepted them as trade-ins on new saddles. Items on consignment will cost more than they would if you bought them directly from the owner, but they will still be less expensive than the same items new. Most tack shops have bulletin boards, and the information posted here can be a good source for horses, trucks, and trailers, as well as clothing and tack.

- Visit boarding stables and look at their bulletin boards. Boarders often advertise items for sale by putting flyers up at their barns.

- Read the classified ads in your local paper and in the back of horse magazines. If you aren't a subscriber, go to the library and look at magazines there.

- Make an "items wanted" flyer that says what you want and how you can be reached. Be precise. If you want a close-contact jumping saddle and your flyer says only "English saddle," you may get calls about dressage saddles and cutback show saddles. If you can, be specific about tree width and seat size. Post the flyers at local stables, tack shops, and feed stores.

- Stores that recycle sports equipment occasionally have riding boots or other gear at reduced prices; and you can sometimes find riding clothes or boots at your local Goodwill or Salvation Army store.

Beyond the Basics: Extra Equipment

Martingales and drop nosebands are popular, but these items are expensive and usually unnecessary. If you ride well and considerately, and your horse is comfortable, healthy, and well-trained, he should not require them. If an uncomfortable bit or a rider's bouncing hands cause a horse to open his mouth or fling up his head in protest, then tying his mouth shut with a noseband, or his head down with a too-short standing martingale, is not the answer.

A neckstrap, on the other hand, is a wonderful steadying element, and an essential item for beginner security. It also provides an emergency "handle" for anyone beginning to jump. A neckstrap is also convenient on the trail, or when training a young horse. You can make your own from a stirrup leather or a piece of soft cotton rope.

Halters and Safety

Your horse will look lovely in a new leather halter with a brass name-plate, especially if the lead matches the halter. But he won't care whether his halter and lead match or whether they are leather, nylon, or cotton. If your halter is sturdy and fits your horse, and your leadrope is unlikely to break, you are well-equipped.

There *is* one occasion when you will need a certain type of halter. Someday, for some specific reason, you may need to leave a horse turned out wearing a halter. The only safe way to do this is to use either a flimsy leather halter (for example, Indian leather, which is clay-tanned and weak, and breaks easily) or a "safety" nylon halter with a thin leather strap for a crownpiece. The "safety" nylon halter is preferable, as the crownpiece is inexpensive and designed to be replaceable. If your horse catches his halter on anything, this halter will break and save him from further danger. There are a lot of "anythings" in the average field—branches, pieces of wood, a broken spot in the fencing, even another horse's tooth.

Rider Clothing

Assuming that you have some show clothing, which is kept clean, tidy, and largely unworn, your main concern will be with items for everyday use. Look for rider clothing the same way you look for tack. You can buy expensive or inexpensive items, new or used, from retail stores, discount stores, or private individuals. As with tack, the best quality is the best bargain, and a used item in good shape is almost always preferable to a cheap new item.

Helmet

Your safety helmet is the single most important exception to the buy-it-used rule. Buy your helmet NEW. Be sure that it meets or exceeds the current ASTM/SEI safety standards, and be sure that it fits well and that the harness is comfortable when fastened. If you fall hard, have it checked *and replaced if necessary*: it will have done its job. Replacing a damaged helmet needn't be expensive. Send your broken or damaged helmet back to the manufacturer. Many manufacturers will replace broken helmets at a reduced price, because examining the damaged ones can help them plan improvements for the next model. Some manufacturers even offer helmets with lifetime warranties.

Take *no* chances with your head. This doesn't mean that you have to spend the maximum; suitable helmets are available in a wide range of styles and prices. Shop around; find one that is safe, affordable, and comfortable. Then *wear* it: for jumping, for dressage, on the trails, everywhere.

Boots

You can often find used boots for sale at local stables. Good used boots are a much better investment than cheap new ones. Cheap tall boots, whether leather or rubber, are often uncomfortable and useless. Cheap leather is either too stiff or too soft, and cheap rubber boots tend to fold in at the front of your ankles and make it difficult and painful to allow your heels to drop. Top-of-the-line Aigle rubber boots, with insulation and steel shanks and leather cuff linings, are not cheap, but their comfort, durability, and versatility are worth the expense. You can wear them for showing, schooling, and mucking out.

Boot prices vary widely. You have many options, from the ultra-expensive custom models to the off-the-rack synthetic ones. If you can't afford reasonable-quality tall leather boots for everyday schooling, buy either good-quality rubber boots or a pair of short boots and a pair of half-chaps. The new Ariat boot system combines comfortable, durable, good-looking paddock boots with leg-hugging half-chaps: the combination is versatile and affordable, and gives the support and overall impression of tall boots.

If money is no object, then you can have the wonderful experience of purchasing custom-made boots, probably from Vogel or Dehner in the United States or Maxwell in England. If you don't want to spend quite that much, you might consider purchasing semi-custom boots from a good manufacturer. Another alternative is someone else's custom boots, adjusted to fit you. Some bootmakers will sell—often at half-price—custom boots that didn't suit or weren't picked up.

Buying boots like this involves a visit to the bootmaker, but it can be well worth the trip. If you find a pair that fits you reasonably well, the bootmaker will make adjustments that will improve the fit and will even put your name inside the boots. Some tack stores offer the same service on custom orders or special orders that were returned or were never picked up in the first place. It's always worth having a look around.

If this is still too expensive, consider purchasing a pair of really *good* rubber boots. The best ones are well-balanced, good-looking, and shaped like a human leg (cheap rubber boots are shaped like a piece of pipe with a foot on one end). They allow you to ride correctly, are comfortable, and, because they are insulated, are not too hot.

Breeches

Contrary to popular opinion, the latest color and style of full-leather-seat German breeches will *not* make you a better rider. If owning them makes you feel wonderful, and if you can afford them, then buy them. But for everyday riding and schooling, any breeches will do—as long as they fit. In fact, breeches aren't even necessary for schooling. Riding jeans are comfortable both for riding and as streetwear, and riding tights are affordable and increasingly popular.

Buy what you like best—it's up to you. You can pay $30 or $300. Buy what fits: try different brands and styles until you find breeches with seams that don't rub and a rise that's the right height for your body.

Few things can interfere with your riding as badly as a pair of breeches whose crotch seems determined to work its way down to your knees. Select material that is comfortable for you, whether it is nylon, cotton, or—in cold weather—polyester fleece. Some materials flatter more than others. Four-way stretch is infinitely flexible, but two-way stretch covers a multitude of sins. Some colors are classic, and others are just for fun. Breeches have recently become available in larger sizes; Dover Saddlery sells them, as does the 18-24 catalog. Maternity breeches and schoolers are also available from Riding Right.

Gloves

Except for the pair you will need for showing, your choice of gloves is entirely up to you and your personal preferences. Riding gloves can be bought for $6 or for $100. Even on a tight budget, you should be able to own a pair for showing and a pair for schooling. Inexpensive work gloves or gardening gloves are nice to have for stable chores, especially if you "do" your own horses and don't want your hands to look as if you spend your weekends burying bones with them.

Stable Stuff

Your grooming kit doesn't need to be elaborate. Hoofpicks are inexpensive if you mark them as yours and keep them for a long time. Store-bought rub rags are expensive; pieces of old towels are free. Your boarding stable should have separate first-aid kits for equines and humans, but it is a good idea for you to have your own, as well as a small portable one for trail rides.

Equipment Storage

Most boarding stables have tack rooms or lockers for boarders' tack. Some will provide space for you to keep a tack trunk as well. If you are renting space in a farmer's field, you may have to keep all your tack and equipment in a trunk. Either way, bigger is better: you want plenty of storage space. Lockers and trunks should be as secure as you can make them—this means solid and locked. This will not protect against the professional tack thief, who will simply cut the locks and take whatever he likes, or load the trunks onto his van to inspect later. Locked trunks keep honest people honest and guard against impromptu borrowing.

More Time, Less Money

Before you buy a new item, try to borrow it first and find out whether you like it in practice. If you think that you want a particular item (bit, reins, noseband, spurs), try to find a friend who owns it and will lend it to you for a few days.

Keeping Track of Your Equipment

Save money, time, and aggravation by not losing equipment. Keep your possessions together, in your tack trunk or locker. Tidiness is a good economy measure: put your things away as you finish using them. Small items are often taken by others—not stolen, just taken, as a result of honest error. Unmarked curry combs, dandy brushes, pulling combs, hoofpicks, and spray bottles all look alike; so do cotton leadropes, navy blue track bandages, and bell boots.

Mark your equipment so that the brush, whip, or leadrope you leave in the crosstie area will still be recognizable as your property when you come back for it. This is especially important if you keep your horse at a large boarding stable, where many riders may own identical items.

Brightly colored plastic tape is an excellent way to mark whips, hoofpicks, scissors, brooms, pitchforks, leadropes, and nylon halters. If you buy the sort of tape you can write on, it will be even more useful. Use your tape or a marking pen—or both—to write your name on the backs of your brushes; if you have more than one horse, write each horse's name on his own brushes. Mark your supplements containers, your oil jugs, your bottle of bute tablets. If you share a barn refrigerator, you can mark your own soft drinks.

Your coolers, quarter sheets, and rugs won't be as easily mistaken for someone else's if you sew your name or initials on them in BIG felt letters. If you are lucky enough to board your horse at a stable where there are washers and dryers for your leg wraps and saddlepads, buy name tags and sew them on everything (remember summer camp? it's the same idea). It eliminates arguments over polo wraps, stable wraps, quilts, and saddle pads.

Equipment in bizarre colors gets "borrowed" less often than equipment in more conventional colors, probably because nobody can possibly confuse your gold-trimmed fuschia sheet with their blue-and-white one. My personal preference is for bright pink. It isn't a classic or elegant color, but it's a very practical one. Although I have lost any number of black whips, navy blue leg wraps, and blue nylon halters over the years, I have *never* managed to lose anything pink. If your horses, like mine, are turned out in muddy fields during the rainy season, you will find that black and brown and even white (a temporary color anyway) splint boots and bell boots disappear quickly in a sea of mud, but you can *always* find the bright pink ones as long as there is even a half-inch edge of boot still visible.

Bizarre colors seem to go on sale more often. Tack shops frequently overstock (and then sell off) their puce or chartreuse halters, but rarely offer any discount on the blue or red ones. Don't be too proud to purchase peculiar colors. I once bought four Bicentennial red-white-and-blue striped halters for less than the price of *one* in a more conventional color; the striped ones were very well-made and lasted for ten years.

Sheets and Rugs

Sheets and rugs can be made to order. Tack and saddlery catalogs tend to offer a set of standard sizes with a few color choices, but there are companies that make nothing but sheets and rugs. If you order from one of these, you will be able to select not just color and trim and piping and monograms, but also material, style of surcingles, neck, fastening, wither design, back design, open/closed/shaped rear, and so forth. If you have a hard-to-fit horse, with high, thin withers, an extra-long back, a long shoulder, or whatever it might be, you should consider this option. The cost, surprisingly enough, tends to be very similar to the prices of good quality off-the-rack items available through major catalogs.

Buy in Bulk

You can buy supplements for your horse in bulk, usually for substantial savings. Team up with others who use the same products, and send off a joint order. It is usually much cheaper to buy a fifty-pound bag of something than ten five-pound bags, and shipping costs are more reasonable for larger orders.

Make Your Own

Another way to get equipment, especially for people who have much more time than money, is to make your own. There are a number of items you can make for yourself and your horse:

- Schooling pads and leg quilts (make patterns from old ones) can be made from old cotton bed pads from the thrift shop.

- Shipping boots aren't beyond the abilities of anyone who can sew a reasonably straight seam: use canvas, denim, or even vinyl; stuff the interior with cotton batting; and add Velcro-type fasteners. You can even line them with fake fleece (remnants are inexpensive).

- If you like the look of fuzzy halter covers, use fleece remnants and Velcro, or buy a yard of fleece in your favorite color.

- The new stretch materials can be used to make helmet covers in colors to match your favorite event shirt.

- If you would like a quarter sheet, make one from an old wool or acrylic blanket.

- For a cooler, use another old blanket. To save annoyance, custom-fit your cooler with Velcro-type fasteners instead of ties and loops.

- If you are good at macramé or braiding, you can buy snaps and use 5/8" cotton rope, thin cord, or even haystrings to create your own stall guards, trailer ties, crossties, and leadropes.

Maintenance: Making It Last

Clean your tack often. Soft, gleaming leather is beautiful at any age; it is also more comfortable for your horse. And well-maintained tack is safer tack: the time you spend cleaning your tack, like the time you spend grooming your horse, allows you to inspect it carefully.

Safety and Comfort

Regular tack-cleaning will keep you aware of the condition of the leather and metal, and safe from unpleasant surprises. You will notice the pits in your snaffle (you thought it was stainless steel, but it was actually chrome-plated) before your horse gets a sore in his mouth. You will notice loose stitching, or cracked and weakened leather, before your reins break. And you will see the fraying elastic on your girth and have it replaced before it gives way.

Economy

Tack-cleaning is also a good way to save money, because properly cared for leather lasts much longer. Leather needs to be treated and conditioned regularly and should be stored in an environment that is well ventilated but neither too humid nor too dry. Too-dry leather can crack, and too-moist leather can mildew; either way, the leather will become weak and unattractive. Avoid wax, silicon, and lacquer products. Leather needs to breathe: it must be able to take in air and let out moisture.

Hard-to-Clean Tack

You don't need to buy plastic scrubbing pads for your really dirty tack. When you pull manes and tails, save the hair. A wad of tail hair makes an effective scrubbing pad. It will save your fingernails as well: horsehair even removes the little greasy "jockeys" that resist all normal sponges.

Toothpaste

After each ride, rinse your horse's bit clean. If rinsing isn't enough, you can scrub your bit safely and inexpensively with a toothbrush (not the one you use on your teeth, though) and toothpaste (most horses like peppermint). Toothpaste is cheaper than metal polish, and if you leave any on the bit—and there is almost always a little residue somewhere, even just a smidgen between the joints of the snaffle—your horse will prefer the taste of toothpaste.

After Every Ride

Whenever you use your tack, clean it. This won't be a full-scale pre-show cleaning, obviously, but at least wipe the leather clean with saddle soap or your favorite leather cleaner/conditioner. Saddle-soap wipes are now available in pop-up containers. You can make your own with an empty container, a stack of cheap terry washcloths or squares cut from an old terry towel, and a large bottle of liquid saddle soap or leather conditioner.

Saddle Pads

Clean your saddle pad often. Washing won't wear it out, but dirt will. Dirt and dust particles grind against the pad's fibers, eventually cutting them and wearing them away. Protect your investment by keeping your equipment clean.

Self-Control: The Ultimate Economy

Beware of buying something just because it is attractive or because someone else has one and you want one, too. Leave the shop, walk around for a few minutes, and ask yourself whether you actually need the item. If you do, go back and buy it. Adults may be less susceptible than children, but we aren't immune to "gotta-have" syndrome.

People who ride cross-country with matching purple shirt, safety vest, helmet cover, pad, overgirth, and polo wraps look very posh, but the horses don't care and neither do the fence judges. It's less expensive and more satisfying to impress the spectators with your performance.

Whether you are a minimalist or a tack junkie, your finances will inevitably dictate some compromises. This should cause no problems as long as you do nothing to jeopardize your physical safety or that of your horse. Economical clothing and good used tack will help your budget without affecting your riding or your horse's performance. And one last thought on tack: hold on to what you have. You may be tempted to sell items that you aren't currently using, but be careful. There seems to be an unwritten rule that as soon as you sell anything, you will acquire a horse who needs the breastplate, boots, or bit that you just sold.

Riding and Schooling Alone

You should be a reasonably competent rider, reasonably secure around your horse, and confirmed in good safety habits, before you take on the challenge of riding and schooling alone. This chapter does not offer how-to-ride basics; that information should be provided by your instructor. It *does* offer information, suggestions, and advice on what to do and what to think about before, during, and after your ride, so that you can make good use of your riding time.

Working Alone

Many adult riders spend a good deal of their riding and schooling time working alone. Some have no choice—their work schedule dictates their riding schedule. Others prefer working alone with their horses and resort to riding very early in the morning or late at night. Many of us have to get along without regular instruction, and all of us work alone between lessons. We know that riding alone can be physically dangerous, and we take safety precautions. But working alone can be dangerous in a different way and can create certain training hazards. It can be difficult to maintain our focus when we work alone. Progress is gradual and incremental, and we have to make a conscious effort to keep our long-term goals in mind. We need to remind ourselves of what we are trying to achieve, and why.

Be Aware of Yourself

Riders who work alone tend to focus exclusively on the horse. They become so concerned with function that they forget the importance of correct form. With no one there to remind them, they can develop sloppy posture, carry their hands unevenly or too low, sit more heavily on one seatbone, or begin dropping or tilting their heads. When you work alone, spend part of each session concentrating on yourself. Make yourself aware of your body position, and try to stay aware of it at all times. If you get the chance to school in an arena with mirrors, watch yourself. You may be amazed at the difference between how you imagined you looked and what you see in the mirror.

If you ride correctly, your schooling will be infinitely more effective. The effort you make to police your own riding—your posture and technique—is well worth the trouble. Correct riding makes the horse more comfortable. A rider who has learned correct basics, and applies them

Arena mirrors can keep you from
falling into bad posture habits.

during every schooling session, makes it easier for the horse to do his job, allows him to do it better and more happily, and teaches the horse to enjoy the time he spends with his rider. Correct riding makes the rider more comfortable, more competent, and more confident.

Correct riding means much more than memorizing specific techniques. It means working to achieve a state of controlled relaxation, both mental and physical, in yourself and in your horse. It means working to achieve suppleness, flexibility, impulsion, and balance in yourself and in your horse. It means acquiring a whole new set of motor skills: how to sit, how to breathe, how to turn your body, how to glance down by dropping just your eyes, not your head. Your lessons may teach you the specific positions and techniques of correct riding, but it is your practice that will determine your progress. If you can use your schooling time to improve your communication with your horse, and to increase his physical ability (and yours), you will progress steadily.

Schooling Sessions

Your schooling time begins long before your ride. From the moment you take your horse from his stall or field, your time together should be quiet and pleasant. You expect your horse to have good stable manners: he should lead, tie and cross-tie; stand quietly; pick up his feet for cleaning; and accept his bridle and saddle calmly. Riders need good stable manners, too. Think in terms of good classroom behavior: no jumping, no running, no yelling, and no hitting. When you work around your horse, always use quiet, slow movements, and stay calm and pleasant. Much of horse-handling, from the ground and from the saddle, has to do with manners and simple courtesy. Many equine bad habits are the direct result of inconsiderate handling. If you can keep things calm and reassuring for the horse on the ground, neither one of you will be upset, tense, or angry when you begin your warmup under saddle.

The Importance of Warming Up

The quality of your warmup will do a lot to determine the quality of your ride or schooling session. Warming up your horse will help him stay sound, but a good warmup can also have a profound effect on the quality of your ride.

Plan a Riding Routine

Here are some suggestions for a riding routine:

- Your horse's warmup begins when you groom him. A thorough grooming will stimulate your horse's circulation and allow you to check him over.

- Mount and walk for 10–15 minutes, encouraging your horse to stretch. Walk on a long rein, then on light contact.

- Spend a few moments in a half-seat or two-point position at the walk, to stretch and strengthen your own legs.

- Warm up at the posting trot. When your horse is quite warmed up and his back is relaxed and swinging, do exercises at sitting trot, posting trot, and in your half-seat.

- Your canter work should incorporate both lengthened and shortened strides.

- Keep the ride interesting for both of you. Practice turns, circles, and any lateral work in your program.

- Finish your ride gently, trotting and walking—your warmup in reverse.

- Groom after riding. You will find any injuries or rubs that might have occurred during the ride, and you will also be certain that your horse is completely cooled out.

Effective Practice

To most people, "natural" means "familiar." Correct riding position will be unfamiliar at first and so will not feel natural. As you learn, as you practice, and as you work alone and accumulate mileage in correct form, what is correct will come to feel more familiar and eventually will feel natural. Practice makes perfect only when the practice is perfect; repeating the same error hundreds of times merely confirms it. Resolve not just to practice but to put *into* practice the skills you learn. Regular, focused repetition of *correct* movements will eventually make it impossible for you to perform them incorrectly.

There are two sayings that will help you practice more effectively: (1) An amateur practices until he can do it right; a professional practices until he can't do it wrong. (2) Amateurs tend to practice what they do well; professionals practice what they don't do well.

While you warm up and cool down, practice what you do well; this is the time to do easier, more familiar things. Some horses, and many riders, get tense and anxious when working on new or unfamiliar movements. The hard work should take place in the middle of your practice session—after you and your horse are thoroughly warmed up, but well before you end your session.

Before each ride, think about what it is you want to achieve, and how you plan to work towards your goals during this session; then ride your plan. But don't be a fanatic—your riding plan isn't carved in stone. Don't try to stick with a set schedule or formula if your horse is having an "off" day, physically or emotionally, or if you are having an "off" day.

Even with no trainer or instructor to guide you, you can make steady progress. Keep your long- and short-term goals in mind, and be satisfied with a little progress at a time. When in doubt, go back to the basics and review your horse's earlier training. You will probably find that somewhere along the line, a lesson was left out or incompletely understood. Going back and filling in gaps is not a waste of time; it's the only way to ensure your progress.

Exercising

The work you do with your horse will determine the sort of muscles he will acquire. Endurance horses, for instance, are encouraged to find their own best ground-covering gait and pace, and then to stay with it. They are tremendously fit, but they don't have the muscle of dressage horses. Dressage puts muscle on horses the way resistance training puts muscle on people: working muscles through various ranges of motion. When you work your horse at gaits other than those he finds easiest, when you take him through all the degrees of extension and collection, what you are doing is bodybuilding.

General Principles of Exercise

Whether you are training for dressage, jumping, eventing, or endurance, some principles apply across the board. Only a relaxed horse can build "good" muscles. Don't force the horse beyond his ability, or beyond his capacity for endurance. Instead of improving, his performance will begin to deteriorate. If you force him to keep going, the strain and fatigue in specific areas of his body will force him to move incorrectly to compensate—just as you do if you have a cramp in a leg or foot, or a blister on your heel, or a pebble in your shoe. In the short term, this incorrect movement can create stresses that may damage your horse. In the long term, the incorrect movement will become a confirmed habit.

Learn the correct sequence of footfalls at each gait, then learn to recognize them from the saddle, by feel. Too many riders who consider themselves "intermediate" or even "advanced," and who speak glibly of extension and collection, are unable to tell where their horses' feet are at any given moment. Some cannot even describe the horse's footfalls at the walk, trot, and canter! If you know exactly where your horse's feet and legs are supposed to be and what they are supposed to be doing at all three gaits, you will be able to school and condition your horse more effectively. You will also be much better able to notice and identify any gait changes or irregularities that could indicate a physical problem or an incipient lameness. Your "feel" will be a valuable asset to your horse's soundness, which should be an important consideration in any schooling or conditioning program.

Conditioning

The best gait for conditioning, especially in the early stages of training, in very cold weather, or with a convalescent horse, is the walk. Think LSD—Long Slow Distance. Indoors or outdoors, in an arena or over terrain, work at the walk will build up your horse without breaking him down. Even if you are preparing for competition, galloping, jumping, and intense upper-level dressage movements should not be practiced day after day. Make a point of changing exercises on alternate days, and give your horse an occasional day of turnout. You won't lose any time; in fact, your horse's strength will improve more quickly if his muscles are allowed 24–48 hours to recuperate between sessions. If turnout is unavailable, you can longe him instead. By longeing your horse, you can build his muscles, improve his gaits, and introduce him to voice commands. Even elementary longeing can give you a safe, effective way to exercise your horse and watch him move at the same time.

Longeing lets you exercise your horse and
watch him move at the same time.

The Stressed Horse

Whatever your schooling program, be careful not to work your horse
too long and too hard, either because you are repeating a success "just
to confirm it" or because something is going badly and you are determined to "get it right." If you work alone, you will have to make a special
effort to notice whether you are pushing too hard. You will certainly
notice if your horse shows depression or overt pain, but watch for the
more subtle signs of overtraining: loss of enjoyment, loss of energy, loss
of sparkle.

The Stressed Rider

Watch for signs of stress in yourself, too. You may be tired, tense, frustrated by people or events at home or at work. Put these feelings aside
before you begin your ride. Groom your frustrations away, warm up your
horse and yourself, and then focus on your work. If you feel your tension building instead of dissipating as you ride, and sense that you are

likely to have a fight with your horse, get off. Even if there aren't many riding days in your week, don't feel pushed to meet an imaginary deadline each time you go to the barn. A good ride can make up for a bad day at work, but a bad day at work followed by a bad ride can make you miserable. Don't set yourself up to fail. If you can't escape your stress, take your horse for a walk—or sit and watch him graze. It's genuine "quality time," and it's cheap therapy.

Making the Most of Available Facilities

Try to do most of your training in a quiet environment so that you and your horse will both be calm and able to pay attention to one another. If your barn offers something for everyone—trails, hills, dressage and jumping arenas, a cross-country course—then you are lucky. But even if it is much less well-equipped, you can find someplace to work.

Work will not always be pleasant or even possible if your only schooling area is outside, but there are certain compensations. Your horse will learn to pay attention to you in spite of distractions, and to cope with a variety of weathers and footings. This will serve you well the next time you take him somewhere else, whether to a show or a forest preserve. If you have access to a trail, even just one that winds around the edge of the property, use it. While enjoying the scenery and fresh air, you can build balance and muscle in your horse without either of you becoming bored.

If you have access to a dressage arena, use it, even if you have no intention of entering your horse in dressage competitions. It offers you a flat area with predictable and even footing; a place in which you may practice straight lines, turns, circles, lateral work, halts, and so on. The dimensions serve as a guide to the size or length of your movements; the markers serve as visual aids.

In the arena or on the trail, share your riding space in safety. Maintain a good following distance, at least two horse lengths away from the next horse. Look ahead, between your horse's ears, at the horse in front of you. If you can see his hind feet, you are at a safe following distance. Some situations are formulas for disaster—avoid them. For example, if a large number of riders from your stable are planning to attend a show

Get your horse used to working on uneven ground . . .

. . . and in all weathers and footings.

on Saturday, do not go to the barn on Friday night with the idea that you will teach your horse something new during rush hour. This is where flexibility comes in. Never mind that this date was marked on your training calendar "begin working on shoulder-in." Do something that your horse already does well, preferably something that he is in the habit of doing well. Doing it well under distracting conditions will be a lesson in itself.

If you have to ride in a crowd, turn the chaos to your advantage. Your horse needs to learn to work quietly among other horses. Use this time to teach your horse to accept other horses passing him from behind and from in front. The presence of those horses will give you a chance to teach your horse to leave the others—or to stand quietly while the others are trotting and cantering.

Avoid Accidents

Make safety a habit, on the ground and in the saddle. Most accidents happen fast, most of them are avoidable, and most of them happen because the rider or horse handler is in a hurry or isn't paying attention. Avoid accidents: be aware, be prepared, and wear your helmet even if you are "just" going for a hack around the pasture. Most accidents happen at home and on the flat, not at competitions or over jumps. *No form of riding is fall-proof.* Every year, it seems, we read about the death or brain injury of another helmetless rider who falls or is kicked while schooling. Arena walls, fence posts, paddock rails, roads, rocks, winter-frozen or summer-baked ground, your horse's hooves—all of these are unforgiving surfaces. Take care of your head; it's not replaceable.

Talking with Your Horse

Take your horse seriously. Every good rider wants to develop a strong bond with her horse, but adults can avoid the typical child's pitfall: thinking of a horse as a furry person whose actions are driven by human emotions. This doesn't mean that you can't love your horse—of course you can. But don't get anthropomorphic. Love your horse by looking after him well. Appreciate and respect him for being a horse, and understand that he is going to think like a horse, not like a person.

Adults can do without the unfortunate attitude that too many children have: *my horse stepped on my foot: he hates me; my horse jumped really well: he loves me.* What your horse needs from you are fairness and consistency. Horses that get praised for no reason, then get punished for no reason, quickly learn to tune out their riders. You want your horse to be tuned in—and that means you need good communication.

Are You a Good Communicator?

Schooling alone, with no instructor to act as interpreter, means that you must be able to communicate clearly and consistently with your horse. Evaluate your skills in this area. How do you communicate with others? Are you a good manager? To ride and train well, you need the attributes of a good manager: you are responsible for all communication, transmissions and receipt, and feedback. A good manager is clear about what is expected, is quick to praise, doesn't criticize needlessly, and, if there is a problem, steers the employee in a new direction instead of saying, "*No, that's WRONG.*" A good manager is a good leader, able to convince, to persuade, and to generate enthusiasm.

Many of these skills can be learned. If you make a conscious effort to pay attention to the information that your horse is giving you as you ride, and make another conscious effort to be more sensitive to what he tells you, you can then make him more sensitive to what you are telling him. In immediate physical terms, this means that during your ride, you will keep your focus by thinking, stride by stride, What does my horse need? What am I doing? Is it working? To be able to do this consistently, you will need to know your horse.

How Well Do You Know Your Horse?

Learn your horse's normal behavior. If he leaps and shies when you first ride him, watch him when he is turned out to play. If he does the same sorts of things—bucking, leaping, shying at nothing—then you will know that this is normal and not a reaction to his tack or his rider.

Be sure that your horse gets enough physical activity. The horse is a large grazing animal, designed to be on the move, albeit slowly, most of the day and night. A well-fed, stall-kept horse will inevitably build up energy—what old-time horsemen called "stall courage"—while he is confined. You may find that your training sessions improve dramatically if you can turn your horse out or longe him before you ride. In either case, your aim is not to "wear him down" or tire him out so that he will offer you exhausted obedience, but to allow him an opportunity to move freely and blow off some steam. By the time you ride, you will have a much better chance of getting his brain into the right gear.

Know your horse's personality, and know how he learns. Horses are individuals. Some learn more quickly and easily than others. Some can be left in a stall for two days and ridden quietly when you finally get to the stable; others will be doing airs above the ground if you are two hours late for your daily ride. Some horses can be coaxed into carrying you past a new and frightening obstacle; others will feel more secure if you dismount and lead them past it a few times. The better you know your horse, the more predictable his behavior will seem.

To work effectively on your own, you must have consideration for your horse and a willingness to recognize in him not just a physical entity but an individual with a soul, a character, aches, pains, moods, and the right to have an occasional bad day.

How many of us can predict an approaching storm, or a change in air pressure, by the ache in a bone or joint? Your horse is affected by weather conditions, by the previous day's activities, by a recent de-worming or a vaccination, by a new set of shoes. Keep his mental and physical state in mind while riding, and be aware of other conditions that may affect his movement and behavior: hard ground, heat, humidity, cold, and wind.

Setting and Meeting Goals

Take your schooling time seriously; respect your riding and the skills you are asking your horse to learn. Riding can be an art as well as a sport. When you work alone, you need to have some goals in mind, some understanding of how to work towards them, and some way to recognize when you have achieved them. Your goals will help you measure your progress, and your satisfaction should come from moving towards each goal, achieving it, and selecting a new goal.

Measuring Your Progress

Short Term: Are you meeting your day-to-day goals?

In chapter 2, you learned how to set and renew your goals. You should work with your instructor on this, as it will help you work efficiently between lessons, even if you have only one lesson each month. It is up to you to define your long-term goal, but once you have done so, your instructor can break it down into several suitable intermediate goals and then set a series of specific, short-term goals for your day-to-day work.

During any given ride, you may have no way of telling how much closer you are to your ultimate goal, but you will know how well you are meeting your short-term goals.

Longer Term: How does your horse look—and how do you look?

Make a point of looking at your horse on a regular basis. Look for general appearance, muscular development, and movement. Your eyes can tell you a lot. Look at your horse in photos, or when he is being ridden by someone else, or while he is turned out in the field. If you are training and riding him properly, he should become stronger, more flexible, more balanced, more responsive, and happier. And he should get steadily better-looking as his muscle structure is built and rebuilt along correct lines. Look at yourself, too; a well-taught rider who makes good use of practice sessions between lessons should also look better as time goes by, both on and off the horse. Regular riding, done correctly, will improve both your posture and your coordination.

The Joy of Flying Solo

When you work with an instructor, you can hand over some of the responsibility. There is someone there to say, "Good, now *stop*" or "Try again, calm down, and now try *this*." When you work alone, with no one to supervise, direct, or interpret, the responsibility is all yours. You must communicate clearly, effectively, and kindly with your horse and give him the chance to succeed. You are in charge, and you have two jobs: to develop your horse's physique, coordination, and skills, and to develop your own.

As an adult, you have the ability to do both. You have maturity and a well-developed attention span. You can be organized—you can plan your ride and then ride your plan. You can be flexible when circumstances don't allow you to do exactly what you had planned to do. You have highly developed language and communication skills, and the ability to apply them to your riding and schooling. You have learned how to learn, and you don't expect your horse's training, or your own riding, to progress in an unbroken upwards line. Most of all, you have the ability to appreciate your horse for the generous, honest, forgiving partner that he is.

It takes a lot of time and a lot of effort to make the change from a sweating and swearing beginner to an accomplished rider, always appearing elegant and effortless. Most of us will never get there; all of us should try. With or without regular instruction, it takes years of work to achieve the balance, suppleness, and "feel" that make up an independent and effective seat. Whether you work alone or under your instructor's supervision, the process of developing a horse's body and mind is a slow one. There is no substitute for correct technique, and there are no shortcuts. Even if you work alone most of the time, you can get where you want to go; it will just take longer. You can see this as discouraging—*years of work?*—or you can see it as a challenge, and a guarantee that you can keep improving forever and that you will never be bored.

The Owner's Role in Health Care

The best gauge of your horse's health and condition is your own know-ledgeable and watchful eye. If you learn what is normal for horses in general and for your horse in particular, you will notice whenever some-thing is *not* normal.

If you look after your own horse, or even visit him daily, you prob-ably notice a lot about him. Even if you aren't consciously aware of it, you already pay attention to his appearance and observe major changes. You can teach yourself to notice the little changes as well, and you can learn to evaluate your horse's condition in just a few minutes—the time it takes to stop by the barn and say goodnight to him.

Evening Visit Checklist

- When you open his stall door, he should come towards the door and face you. When he looks at you, his eyes should follow you, and they should be open and clear.

- His ears should be warm, and they should follow his eyes—forward if he is looking straight at you.

- His coat should be shiny and flat, even in winter (if he is out-doors in the cold, his coat will be fluffed up but should still be shiny).

- When you pet him, his skin should feel pliable and easy to move over the bones and muscles underneath. If his skin feels tight— hidebound—he may be dehydrated.

- If he has a heavy winter coat, run your thumb along his ribcage. If you can just detect his ribs, fine. If your thumb bounces from rib to rib, your horse is too thin.

- When he breathes on you, his breath should smell sweet. If it isn't, have the vet check his teeth.

- When you run your hands over his legs, you should find no swellings or heat.

- Look at his droppings. You should see a pile of moist, formed balls; if they are hard and dry, loose and unformed, or smell bad, something is wrong.

- If there are *no* droppings in a stall that was cleaned twelve hours ago, it isn't a good sign. Horses are designed to eat, digest, and excrete around the clock.

- If you take him out of his stall and turn him out or handwalk him, he should move evenly.

- While he is moving, his tail should be carried away from his body, not clamped down.

- Notice his behavior. Does he seem normal? If his feed tub is always licked clean by five-twenty, you should worry if he still has grain when you drop by to see him at eight. This is a danger signal. Inspect him closely and call the vet.

Nutrition

Your horse's feeding program will depend on a number of factors: the types and amounts of feeds provided by the stable, the condition of the pasture, the amount and type of exercise he gets each day. You will need to work with your barn manager and your veterinarian to create an individual feeding program for your horse.

Items you need should be kept close at hand.

Grooming

Your grooming kit may be spartan: a dandy brush, a body brush, a hoofpick, and a curry comb, or it may be elaborate. What you have is less important than how you use it and what you learn as you use it. Grooming does much more than clean your horse; it offers you a daily opportunity to check him over. Grooming your horse helps you to become familiar with what is normal for him. As you groom, you will notice any skin problems, scrapes, cuts, sores, sensitive areas, swellings, and bruises. If you groom thoroughly every time you ride, you will notice changes in your horse's legs, such as heat in a joint or a slightly mushy tendon.

Professional Help

You are not the only one who cares about your horse's health and performance; you have professionals on your side. Your veterinarian and farrier care about your horse's health. So does your instructor, and so does your barn owner or stable manager. These people probably won't come up to you and volunteer information. They will be glad to answer questions, but they will wait to be asked. Don't hesitate to ask questions. Many professionals have learned the hard way that some horse owners don't really want detailed answers to their questions. If you want more than a brief general answer, say so.

Part of your job as a horse owner is to become knowledgeable about horse care. Never worry about asking stupid questions; never be afraid to ask. Never be embarrassed to admit your ignorance, never be ashamed to say "I don't know what that means" or "I don't understand" or "Could you explain that, please?"

Ignorance has several forms:

1. Things you know you don't know.
2. Things you don't know you don't know.
3. Things you think you know but you don't know.

Ignorance is *not* bliss. The consequences of ignorance can hurt your horse. Horse abuse is not limited to angry acts of physical violence; ignorant neglect ("But we did have his feet trimmed, just last year!") and inappropriate expressions of love (an extra bucket of grain for "being good") can be equally dangerous.

There is only one stupid question: the one you don't ask.

Prevention is better, and usually cheaper, than cure. Use your intelligence and your professionals' advice to take good preventive care of your horse. Work with them to develop a complete management plan, integrating your horse's environment, his activities, and his health care—everything that affects his life and his health.

Evaluate Your Source of Information

As adults, we can expect, even demand, to be taken seriously by other adults. When we ask questions, we are unlikely to be told "Just do it" or "Because I say so." If we are offered such answers, we don't have to accept them; we can look for someone who gives better answers.

As adults, we have learned to recognize the signs of professional competence even if we are ignorant about the subject area.

A competent professional will demonstrate quiet confidence, will be able to answer questions simply, and will offer explanations that are just as deep and complex as you want. If a competent professional does not know the answer to a question, you will hear "I don't know" or, even better, "I'll find out." Good veterinarians, farriers, and instructors are happy to expound on the principles and techniques of their art. If someone offers you vague or unsatisfactory answers—"That's just the way horses are" or "Well, horses get like that sometimes"—thank that person politely and look for another source of information.

If your horse lives in your backyard or in a rented field, your veterinarian and farrier may be your only support professionals. If he lives at a stable run by a competent, caring manager, you have another professional on your team. Your stable manager will see your horse often, probably more often than you do. This person will be able to help you and your horse *and* make decisions on your behalf in your absence: whether there is something seriously wrong with your horse, and whether to call the veterinarian or farrier.

Routine health care usually includes vaccinations, deworming, teeth floating, and sheath cleaning. Your stable manager can hold your horse during these twice-yearly calls, but try to be there yourself. These visits give you the unusual opportunity to talk with your veterinarian when there isn't an emergency.

The Pain-Depression Connection

In horses, pain frequently presents as depression. A horse with a bowed tendon or a huge bleeding cut on the leg may limp but will probably eat dinner anyway. A horse with incipient colic or another illness may seem quiet, subdued, tired, inattentive, and not very hungry. If this happens to your horse, watch him closely and be ready to call your veterinarian. Whatever is wrong may be something that can be stopped before it gets too serious. A "too quiet" horse shouldn't be taken lightly. Something is wrong, it may already be serious, and it is not a mood swing. Colic is not just a tummyache or a "Maalox moment"; it's the leading cause of death in horses.

Emergency Vet Care

When you call the vet, speak slowly and clearly. What you say will make a difference to his schedule and driving speed. Don't cry "wolf" and make him burn rubber on the way to your barn if your horse has a scrape and is missing some hair. But if your horse is bleeding badly or in mid-colic, say so. The more accurate your description, and the more complete your information, the better prepared your vet will be to deal with the situation.

Telephone Procedure

Have some basic facts ready, written down if possible. If your vet is out on another call, you may have to talk to an answering service. The urgency of your emergency will have to be conveyed by the *facts*.

First say who you are, where you are, and give your telephone number. If you are disconnected, they will still be able to tell the vet where— if not what—the emergency is. They will ask:

1. Why did you call? Explain what the problem is (injury? illness?). If you are talking to an answering service, you will probably be asked whether it is an emergency. You can say "Yes," "No," or "I'm not sure." The answering service will contact the vet, who will telephone you and ask for additional information.

2. How long ago did it happen? If you found the horse bleeding or in mid-colic an hour after feeding time, it probably happened within that hour, or someone would have noticed then. If you found him just before breakfast, it could have happened anytime after dinner the night before.

3. What are his vital signs, and how do they compare to his normal TPR? This information can help your vet determine the horse's status. You should check these and *write them down* before you ring the vet. The following values are average for the generic horse, but you should know what is normal for your particular animal.

   Temperature: 99–100.5°F   An elevated temperature can mean inflammation or infection; a low temperature could indicate shock.

Resting Pulse: 32–44   It helps if you know your horse's normal resting pulse. A high resting pulse indicates internal stress. Stand on his left side with your watch in your left hand, and put the middle finger of your right hand on the artery running along the inner side of your horse's jaw. Count the pulse for fifteen seconds (watch the second hand); then multiply by four. Don't use your thumb; your own pulse will interfere with your counting.

Respiration: 8–20   Is your horse having trouble breathing, or is he panting? A resting horse will normally breathe about twelve times per minute. Watch your horse's flank move in and out (one in-and-out movement equals one breath), and count his number of breaths per minute. Again, count for fifteen seconds and multiply by four.

CRT (Capillary Refill Time)   Press a finger against your horse's gum, then count the seconds as the white spot becomes pink again). It should take one to two seconds at most; any longer, and the horse is low on body fluids. Gums any color other than pink (pale, yellow, red, blue, or purple) indicate serious trouble. Tell your veterinarian immediately.

Dehydration   Check for dehydration by pinching the skin on the point of your horse's shoulder. It should snap back into place as soon as you let it go. If it stays elevated for two to three seconds, your horse is moderately dehydrated. If it takes six seconds or longer to flatten, your horse is severely dehydrated.

A note on temperature: if your horse's temperature seems excessively high, *you may not have remembered to shake down the thermometer.* Shake the thermometer down, and take his temperature again. You may be pleasantly surprised.

Appearance

Does your horse stand or move differently? Do you see any obvious injuries: wounds, swellings, "hot spots"? Do his eyes have a "worried" look? New wrinkles over the eyes indicate pain. Does his coat look different—sweaty, dry, or sticking out instead of lying flat?

Behavior

What is your horse doing? Is he eating and drinking normally? Is he restless or agitated—is he pawing? Is he lying down when he would normally stand? Is he looking or biting at his sides?

While You Wait for the Vet

While the vet is on the way, try to make your horse comfortable. This might mean grooming or blanketing him, or leaving him alone in a dark stall. Don't medicate him unless the vet suggests it: painkillers and tranquilizers can make it harder for your vet to make an accurate diagnosis.

If bleeding is the problem, use a direct pressure bandage to stop it. Don't panic if there is a lot of blood, especially from a lower-leg wound; a 1,000-pound horse can lose enough blood to paint a large wall (up to 2 gallons) before blood loss becomes a serious problem.

If colic is the problem, don't wear the horse out by walking him endlessly. If he is standing quietly, put him in a stall and leave him alone. But if he wants to roll or thrash about whenever you let go of him, keep him walking.

If an eye injury is the problem, treat it as an emergency. Horses are very susceptible to eye injuries. An untreated or incorrectly treated injury can lead to infection, permanent damage, loss of vision, or loss of the eye. Don't try to treat it yourself; unprescribed ointments can do more harm than good.

Write It Down

Keep your pencil and paper handy, and think about everything your vet might need to know. If you write everything down as it comes to you, you will be able to supply the vet with information that may help him arrive at a faster, more accurate diagnosis.

Have there been any changes to your horse's routine lately—is anything different? Is your mare in heat? Mention any *feed changes* (amount or type of feed, time of feeding), any *social changes* (has a new horse been turned out with yours? has an old friend been taken away?), any *physical changes* to equipment (new bit? new saddle?) or shoeing (lameness from a too-short trim or a change of angle).

Working with Your Veterinarian

If you can, be there when your vet arrives. (You may have to call in sick at work to do this. Hard experience has taught many horse owners not to expect horse emergencies to be taken seriously by their employers.) Your veterinarian knows horses, but only you know how your horse has been doing, how he feels, and what's been going on with his training. Your veterinarian knows what is normal for the species, but you know what is normal for this individual.

Groom the horse first. You're not preparing for a show, and the horse will almost certainly be put into his field or his stall as soon as the vet has finished with him. But groom the horse anyway, for several reasons. A clean, groomed horse is easier to evaluate and work on. Cleaning a spot for an injection should take a few seconds with a piece of cotton and some alcohol, not ten minutes with a hammer and chisel. It's hard to feel for damage, or even heat and swelling, in a leg that is crusted with layers of mud. Many horses feel insecure when they are ill or injured and find gentle grooming reassuring. One of my mares becomes extremely affectionate when she is ill; her normal behavior is much less tractable. If she gets too sweet and docile, I take her temperature.

Even if your horse is torn and bleeding, don't panic. If you can stay calm and hold the horse, it will help the vet. If you are too upset, stand back and let someone else do it; your emotions will excite your horse, just when he needs to be calm and quiet.

When you ask your vet for advice, *take it.* Nothing is more frustrating for a professional, be it your instructor, your farrier, or your veterinarian, than to have someone request their advice, pay their fee, and then do nothing.

Pay promptly. Write the check the day the bill arrives. If the groceries are a little sparse that week, or if the credit card company gets paid the minimum—too bad. As a horse owner, your priority should be clear. Your vet is not a corporation, a credit banker, or a charity. Everything he does is hands-on, on his own time, and he is out of pocket for the drugs and treatments he dispenses. And believe me, the people from the grocery store and the credit card company are never going to get up in the middle of a cold night and drive very fast on bad roads just so that they can pump oil into your horse's stomach or sew up a torn leg.

First-Aid Kit

Horses get hurt at home and away from home. You have a first-aid kit at the barn, but what if your horse gets hurt at a show, or in the trailer, or while you are out riding on a trail? You need a first-aid kit for your trailer—less elaborate than the one you have at the barn—and you need a small first-aid kit for trail rides (keep it in a belt bag), with a few basic essentials. Don't forget that first aid is just that: *first* aid. The contents of your kit shouldn't duplicate the contents of your veterinarian's office or van. A first-aid kit enables you to deal on the spot with *minor* injuries: scrapes, small cuts, and so on. But that isn't all. If your horse has a serious injury, you aren't going to fix it yourself, but the contents of your first-aid kit should enable you to stabilize your horse and keep the bleeding under control until the veterinarian arrives.

First, you'll need a box. Almost anything will do, as long as it is waterproof and portable. If it's going on the trail with you, it had better be small and light, but if it is going to be kept in your trailer, it can be quite a bit larger—and if it is going to be a permanent fixture in your barn, it can be very big indeed. Whatever you use should be instantly identifiable as a container for medical supplies: if you use red plastic tape (or white on a red box) to make a cross on the top of your container, you can send anyone back to your tack room or trailer and know that they will find the correct box.

Your first-aid box should contain some basic items:

Thermometer (with string and clip)

Watch (with second hand)

Vaseline (tubes being most convenient)

Cleansing towels (Wet Wipes or similar)

Antiseptic cleaning solution

Wound powders, ointments, and sprays

Saline solution

Ophthalmic antibiotic ointment

Bandage materials (Vetrap or similar)

6-inch gauze rolls

4 × 4 gauze squares

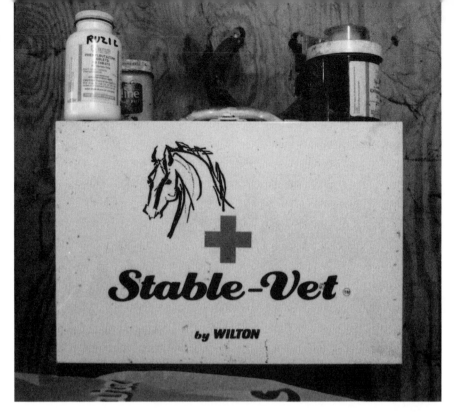

Your equine first-aid kit should be
easy to locate and identify.

Sheet cottons

Duct tape

Bandage cutter or blunt-tipped scissors

Stethoscope

Tape to the inside of the lid of your first-aid box:

A record of your horse's normal TPR, and of the normal range

temp: 99–100.5

resting pulse: 32–44

respiration: 8–20

CRT: 1–2 seconds at most (if longer, the horse is low on
body fluids).

Telephone numbers of local veterinarians and the nearest
veterinary hospital

A list of everything in the box

A more elaborate box might include everything listed above, plus the following:

Adhesive tape

Betadine

7% iodine

Ichthamnol

Rubbing alcohol

Hydrogen peroxide

Bute

Aspirin

Banamine injectable

Antibiotic injectable

Syringes and needles (narrow for banamine, wider for penicillin)

Barn towels

Twitch

Stick for tourniquet

Clippers

Fluorescein strips

Ziploc plastic bags (when filled with ice, can be used as cold packs)

On the Road

A mild tranquilizer is a useful thing to have with you when you travel, in case horse or trailer problems require that you unload your horse on the road. Check with your vet in advance: find how much of what tranquilizer to use (and under what conditions) on your particular horse, and then carry it with you.

In the tack compartment of your trailer, along with your first-aid box, you should have money for pay phones, and a list of veterinarians and telephone numbers along your route.

The *Hawkins Guide to Horse Trailering on the Road* is especially helpful; there should be a copy in the glove box of every towing vehicle.

More Money than Time

If you can afford to pay for a complete care package at a posh boarding stable, you won't have to deal with the veterinarian or the farrier yourself; the stable staff will do it for you. This kind of service costs more, but if your time is the most precious commodity you have, and you need to save your limited time at the stable for riding, it may suit you best.

Some Money, Some Time

You can save money by spending money: a healthy horse requires less vet care. Routine medical care can be planned for and worked into your budget. This includes deworming, vaccinations, and dental care. Timely immunizations mean fewer illnesses. Deworming the horse on a regular schedule and having his teeth floated when they need it means that the feed you buy won't be wasted.

More Time than Money

Consider keeping your horse outdoors. You will spend more time grooming him, but well-maintained outdoor horses have better physical and mental health, fewer respiratory and foot problems, and better feet. Living outdoors also meets the horse's requirements for movement, light, and social contact.

Vet Bills and Medical Supplies

There may be some flexibility in your vet bill. If you usually pay to have your horse dewormed by tube twice a year, in addition to your administration of paste wormers in between the vet's visits, you might consider using paste year-round. Talk to your vet, and ask him what he recommends; tell him that you want optimum health for your horse at the minimum price. He will understand and will probably have suggestions.

Use catalogs to best advantage when you purchase supplies. Gauze bandages, syringes and needles, feed supplements, medications, paste wormers, and so on—all are cheaper if you buy them through vet supply catalogs. These items are cheaper still if you make a bulk purchase, ordering six of this and a dozen of that and a case of the other.

You may have to enlist some friends to share the order, but postage and handling charges for a large order are negligible when divided among three or four people, and the reduction in costs makes the extra effort worthwhile.

Commercial cold wraps and ice boots are costly. Keep a few bags of frozen peas on hand, instead. A bag of frozen peas is flexible, conforms to leg contours, and can be refrozen and used as a cold pack again. If you plan to use them again, put the entire bag into a large Ziploc freezer bag and mark it clearly so that you won't accidentally cook those peas for your family's dinner. Unlike the original bag, it won't explode and scatter frozen veggies all over the barn aisle if you drop it.

There are commercial hot packs and wraps on the market, but you can make your own with bran, water, and another Ziploc bag. Select the size bag you prefer and heat it in the microwave (leave it open until it's hot) to create a hot pad that is cheap, easy, and can be reheated. It can also be recycled: if you don't want to reuse it, you can feed it to your horse when you have finished the hot-pack session and the bran is merely warm.

Bandages

If your horse injures a leg and requires a bandage to cover a treatment pad, old socks can be very helpful. Save your old sports socks, cut off the feet and you will have two pull-on leg bandages. If your horse injures his neck or even his head, part of a leg from an old pair of panty hose can be pulled over the head and neck to cover the treatment pad. The mesh allows air to circulate, and the bandage can be left on for quite a long time. With a couple of panty hose legs and a box of stick-on sanitary pads, even a wound on the side of the neck can be treated and covered again with a minimum of time and trouble.

Recordkeeping

Wherever you keep your horse, you should keep a complete file on him. The file will include all the information that anyone could possibly need to identify your horse and understand his entire medical and dental history. You may be able to recite it all from memory, but write it down anyway and leave a copy wherever your horse lives. This file will make life much easier for your veterinarian, and it may save your horse's life someday. If he is injured or ill and neither you nor your regular veterinarian can be reached, a veterinarian who is unfamiliar with your horse will be called in. At the very least, this record will provide him with information that can make a significant difference to the ease and safety with which he can diagnose and treat your horse. Your horse's complete file would include a copy of his papers (if any) or a description of his height, age, sex, breeding, color, and markings and a set of identifier photos (front, back, and side views).

Your Horse's Medical Record

You should maintain a complete medical record for your horse. You know his normal TPR; put that in the record in case someone else should need it. The record should also show your horse's schedule of immunizations and boosters, his deworming schedule, and what product was used. It should also list any special medical care he may have received for illness or injury. The record should include—highlighted, starred, or circled in red—any allergies that your horse has. This would include allergic reactions to medicine (specify which dewormer, or which oral or injectable drug). If your horse has had a strong local reaction to certain shots, note the fact and also note that those medications should be not be administered in his neck. A sore bottom may cause him to walk oddly for a day or two but won't cause lasting damage; a sore and swollen neck may keep him from drinking, which can be much more serious.

The medical record should show everything that has been done with your horse—and when. If you have a gelding or a stallion, the records should show how often his sheath has been cleaned and whether any tranquilizer was needed.

If you own a brood mare, keep a record of her blood type, a record of her cycles, and information about her breeding history (previous foals, number of covers, length of gestation period, and any notes about the foaling process itself).

Detailed shoeing information is an important part of the record. A farrier who is not familiar with your horse might be called in an emergency, and detailed records would be invaluable to him.

If your horse has any stable vices, they should be part of the record. If there is anything else that someone handling him might need to know—for instance that he does not cross-tie—include that information as well.

Include specific feeding instructions. List everything that makes up your horse's diet, including the amounts. Include any seasonal or other changes in your feeding program, and be sure to describe any supplements you feed, including their composition and amounts.

Health Papers

At many stables, you will not be permitted to take your horse off the trailer, much less bring him into the barn, until you have produced recent health papers and a current negative Coggins. The same papers are required for a horse travelling between states. Health papers are not a complete medical record, but they indicate that the horse is current on his vaccinations and deworming, and that he has recently been seen by a veterinarian.

To a great extent, you are the person responsible for your horse's health. For your horse's sake, call early and enlist professional help to solve a medical problem before it gets worse. And for the sake of your finances, realize that an emergency call made early on will be much less expensive than a series of calls made later.

A medical colic caught early and treated from its onset may remain a medical colic; a neglected medical colic may become a surgical colic— or a death sentence. My own rule of thumb is this: I would rather be told, nine times out of ten, that I was overly concerned, than to be told, one time out of ten, that I ought to have called earlier when something could still have been done.

Euthanasia

It isn't easy to let go. We're not good at this, as a species: we want to hold on to the animals and to the people we love. We will use extreme measures, do whatever it takes to prolong any spark of life as long as we possibly can.

As adults, we may have seen grandparents, parents, even contemporaries die; you will, no doubt, have attended the funerals of family members. And by this time in your life, you have probably lost a beloved cat or dog, or even a horse. You know what the pain of loss is like, and you want to do whatever you can to avoid experiencing that pain again. Nobody ever wants to put down a much-loved animal that is a friend and companion. But sometimes the best thing we can do for the horse we love is to let him go.

Since pain in horses tends to present as depression, if we persist in thinking in human terms we can convince ourselves that the horse is "sad" or perhaps apprehensive about death. Not so. A depressed, "sad-looking" horse is a horse in pain, and a horse living entirely in the painful present. A horse doesn't think about how wonderful the past was or worry about whether he will be cured or dead in a week—all he knows is that he hurts, *now*. We are the ones who tend to hold on too long, because we can remember past pain and anticipate the future pain of losing our horse.

We make decisions, major and minor, for our horses throughout their lives—where they live, what they eat, what they do. We determine when and whether to breed them, what sort of shoes and saddles and bits they will wear, what sort of training program and competition schedule they have. Our decisions determine what kind of lives our horses live, and what quality of life they have.

Putting a horse down is, literally, the last thing we want to do. But sometimes it is what we have to do—it's our last obligation, our final responsibility to our equine partner. We don't have the right to avoid our responsibilities and put off our last decision while the horse stands there in pain and we hope for a miracle. We "play God" all the way through our horses' lives, not just at the very end. And while making the decision to put a horse down isn't easy, it is easier than living with the knowledge that we kept a horse alive—and suffering—for too long, just because we couldn't bear to let him go. If you have given your horse a good life, be strong enough to give him a good death if you must.

Competitions and Clinics

Competitions can be a good way to have fun, improve your horse, and see how your training is coming along. Good preparation can make the difference between a satisfying experience and a frustrating one. When you select a competition, keep several things in mind:

- The type and level of competition (dressage? hunter? event?)

- The distance and travel time involved

- The cost (travel expenses, entries, stabling, motel or camp-ground)

- The competition's reputation (is it safe and well-managed?)

Be equally systematic when selecting classes. You will need to know:

- How each class is judged

- What is expected of you in terms of riding and clothing

- What is expected of your horse in terms of grooming and tack

If you haven't been to a particular type of competition before, or if you haven't been to any sort of show for a long time, attend one as a spectator. Watch carefully, and find out exactly what is expected of horse and rider. If you "do" your own horse, you might want to attend a show as a groom. This will let you find out exactly how much and what sort of work you will need to do when *you* show.

Types of Competitions

Dressage shows will help identify any holes or weak spots in your riding and training. Dressage tests are designed to show the judge—and you—whether you are training your horse correctly. You can go to a dressage competition and have safe fun, even if you haven't a lot of time to ride or can't ride very often. It's easier for your horse, too. At the lower levels, he won't need the sort of condition and muscle that would allow him to event, show jump, or "do the hunters" safely.

Hunter shows give you an opportunity to test your smoothness, co-ordination, and the quietness of your aids. Hunter shows aren't just for riders at hunter barns; they can be useful for event riders, too. Many lower-level event riders lack finesse; hunter shows remind them to ride quietly, set up the horse, and allow him to jump smoothly.

Eventing isn't all "three ways, three days." There are two-day and even one-day events; you will be able to find competitions that suit your

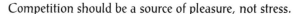

Competition should be a source of pleasure, not stress.

budget, your schedule, and your riding level. Even a schooling event, where the jumps may be only two or two-and-a-half feet high, will let you test yourself, your horse, and your training in three separate disciplines.

Preparation

Most working riders can't afford the time or money to attend a lot of competitions. Give yourself an advantage: prepare as well as possible so that you will enjoy the day and get the most from the experience. While you are at a show, especially if you are a spectator, watch and evaluate every horse and every rider. Which riders do you admire? Which ones appear smooth, calm, well-prepared? What are they doing—or not doing? Use the insights you gain when you take your own horse to a show.

Competition as Stimulus

Competitions shouldn't be cause for unpleasant tension, constant worry, or a stress level that makes you sick. Competitions should be enjoyable for both horse and rider. If you come prepared and relaxed, competing can become a form of low-stress entertainment. Instead of making you sick, your "competition nerves" will give you a feeling of pleasurable excitement. Instead of being tense and short of breath, you will simply feel intensely aware of yourself, your horse, and your surroundings.

Showing Realities

Maximize your enjoyment and minimize your stress by taking a realistic approach to showing. Don't go to a competition planning to battle for a trophy against riders whose trainers take them and their various horses to shows every weekend. You aren't there to kill yourself trying to beat the people on the circuit. This doesn't mean that you go with a defeatist attitude—you intend to show the very best that you and your horse can do. But if you aren't going head-to-head with the circuit regulars, how can you compete?

It's easy. First, you should compete with *yourself*. Your ambition at shows should be the same ambition you have when you are schooling at home: *you want to improve*. Do something that tests you and your horse, and do it better than you did last time. You'll be a success, whatever the color of the ribbon—or even if there isn't a ribbon!

You can compete with the course: you and your horse are competing as a team against the course designer. You can compete with your previous record. If you've never managed to get your horse over a water jump, and this time he ignores the plastic ducks and clears it, takes it in stride, that's a success. If your horse jumped a ditch without stopping to inspect it for dragons, then you have achieved a personal victory, even if you trotted up to it and levitated over it, and even if you finished with time faults. You can have success *regardless of results*.

Success

You want to be successful—that goes without saying. But before you leave home, decide what "success" means to you, at this show, with this

Keep your focus on the effort, not the results.

horse, on this day. Success is individual, personal, and subjective. One rider's idea of success might be winning a High Point trophy; another rider's might be getting around a particular cross-country course; someone else's dream might be to complete a jumping class without going off-course. For every rider who will be bitterly disappointed if the day ends without a blue ribbon, there is another rider who will be thrilled to get a ribbon of any color.

A good day at a show is a success, with or without ribbons. A good day is one during which nobody gets hurt, the horses and riders enjoy the competition and learn something, and a good time is had by all. Performance at the show is a secondary consideration; ribbons and trophies make nice souvenirs but are a distant third. When you compete, try to remember that "showing" means just that. You have worked hard to train and condition yourself and your horse; now you have the chance to show a judge how correct your training has been, how well your horse is going, how lovely he looks, and how subtle your aids are.

The Adult Advantage

Although it sometimes takes strong talk on the instructor's part, especially to riders who collected trophies as children, adults can usually bring their maturity to bear on the situation. One advantage to being an adult is that you don't have to confuse results with performance. We all like to have our efforts rewarded—or at least recognized. But most children, while on course or in the ring, think about how they are *doing*. Adults, on the other hand, can learn to think about how they are *riding*, and keep their real, long-term goals in mind.

Judges: Friends or Foes?

You may have heard that a particular judge dislikes certain breeds and won't place them, but consider the source of the information before you decide to stay at home. For every judge who supposedly "hates Arabs/Morgans/Quarter Horses/Appaloosas" or who "won't place anything under sixteen hands," there may be a disgruntled competitor who simply did not perform well in front of that judge. If our success depends on ribbons and we don't get them, we tend to look for someone to blame.

Riding can make you feel complete: you can ride just
for the joy of communication with horses. With or
without a ribbon, a good ride is a success.

It's much easier to make the judge responsible for our low scores than
to take a long hard look at our own riding and training program.

Don't avoid showing because you are worried that the judges will
be unfair. Most judges try to be fair; they are there to help you, to tell
you what you do well and what you need to do better. If a particular

show fits into your schedule—right distance, right dates, good venue—then go there. Whether you win, place, or just participate, you will learn something. If you can focus on correct training and good riding instead of worrying about whether a particular judge will like your horse's breed, your saddle, or the cut of your riding coat, you can relax, ride better, enjoy yourself more, and get a better result.

If you actually do show in front of an unfair judge, so what? It's one judge at one show, and it isn't the end of the world. Yes, you will be disappointed, but you already know that life isn't always fair. If you had a good ride and feel that your riding and training are improving, you will be happy regardless of your placing.

Your relationship with your horse is what matters, and that has nothing to do with shows or judging. You may get a low score, but it won't undermine the affection and respect you have for your horse.

Someone to Watch Over You

Even if it's just a one-day schooling show, don't go to a competition alone if you can possibly avoid it. And if you are sharing a trailer with another competitor, don't go with someone who will disappear into the beer tent or go off to visit friends as soon as you arrive, leaving you with both the horses and all the work. Take someone with you who is *not* competing and who will help you: a spouse, a child, a friend. Your stress level at a show will be much lower if you know that someone is there to help you. Even if you are ultra-efficient and can do it all on your own, take someone with you. If nothing else, that person can bring you food, tell you how nice you look, and remind you that you are there to have a good time.

Horse Show Food

Adults, unlike children, are often less than thrilled with the food generally available at horse shows. The prices are high, and the quality is uneven at best—and can be dreadful. Many children seem to have cast-iron stomachs—perhaps they are just accustomed to school food?—and don't seem to be affected by the standard horse show fare, which is traditionally composed of equal parts cholesterol and caffeine. Adults don't do well with this sort of diet. The typical high-fat, high-salt, something-in-a-bun meal can cause them to be dry-mouthed and jittery at the show, and experience puffy hands and slow thinking the next morning at work.

Bring a cooler—a big one. Fill it with finger foods (if you are holding a horse, you may have to eat with one hand). Pack lots of fruit and vegetables—if you don't eat all your carrot sticks or apples, your horse will be happy to help you out. Take mineral water, juice, a sports drink, some soft drinks if you like them—and a lot of ice. Take a few extra plastic bags. With these and some ice, you can make cold packs for humans or equines.

Make Each Competition a Positive Experience

Your horse will be more excited at a show. You must take this into account, and allow him to be more nervous, curious, and active. It's natural. Behaviors that are not permitted at home—biting, kicking, hysterical bucking on the longe line—cannot be permitted at a show either, but a certain amount of high-headed inattention is to be expected, especially if your horse hasn't been to many shows. The same holds true if you haven't shown much, because you too will be nervous, curious, and distracted.

First Time Out: Don't Compete

If you have a new horse, or a horse that is new to shows, then go to a show and don't compete. Just hack around the grounds, or handwalk him if he is truly nervous. Horses can't cope with too many new things at once—and if your own nerves are on edge, your horse will be frantic. If your horse worries about strange trailers, rustling trees, billowing tents, buzzing loudspeakers, or even the killer cows in the pasture next to the arena, don't wait until competition day to find out. Deal with these things when neither of you is feeling pressured.

Spend the entire day wandering around with your horse on a long rein, feeding him treats and making reassuring noises. With no competition nerves, no frantic schedule, and no pressure to perform, you will be able to take your horse home in a relaxed state after a pleasant day out. Next time, those things will be "old" and acceptable to your horse. The "new" part will be the competition itself, the arena, the judge's box, the flowers, the jumps, and perhaps your own nervousness as well (don't expect your horse to adapt to all the changes at once).

Competing

Plan your arrival time on the grounds. Allow yourself plenty of time to calm the horse down. You can do this by longeing him (*if* longeing is part of your regular routine at home) or by riding him around the show grounds. If he seems too worried to be reliable under saddle, you can handwalk him around the grounds for an hour or so (use your longeing cavesson instead of your halter for better control). When your horse has seen and heard and smelled everything, he can begin to get bored; when he begins to get bored, he will begin to get calm. At home, you try to keep your horse interested; away from home, it's quite nice to have a bored horse. When you are in the ring, create a positive experience for him. Your horse can't shine if he's frightened of you. If he makes a mistake and you punish him, he isn't going to want to go in that ring again and perform when you bring him back for your next class.

Do What You Know

Don't try to teach your horse anything new at a competition. The unfamiliar surroundings, sights, and sounds are exciting and distracting. If you ask him to do only what he does at home, and he does it well in spite of the distractions, you should be pleased. If you are lucky enough to have your instructor or coach with you, take your cue from her: a good coach won't try to teach you anything new on the day of the competition. She will just try to keep you organized, calm, and doing your best to show how well you can do what you have been practicing. Treat your horse the way a good coach would treat you.

For the same reason, it is preferable to work to a higher level at home than at the show. The new jump height or lateral movement you are beginning to school at home should be left at home until it is part of your routine work. In fact, if either you or your horse is nervous or new to showing, you should actually drop back a little at the show and do only those things that the horse does very well at home.

Competition Nerves I: The Road Worrier

If competition nerves are a major problem, start small. If your own boarding barn holds a small competition, participate in that. It's an ideal introduction to showing, with minimum stress on horse and rider; your horse can go back into his own stall between classes, and you know where all the bathrooms are.

If the first, at-home show goes well for you, look for a few small one-day schooling shows close to home. If you are worried about taking your horse away from his home barn, this will be an ideal introduction to showing away from home. You'll probably know most of the other riders, and you won't have to trailer for hours to get there, or stay overnight. This can be a good way to begin showing in a casual, informal, friendly atmosphere. Once you are comfortable competing at local schooling shows, look for a local rated show—or consider going to a more distant venue.

Competition Nerves II: The Adrenaline Junkie

If you are aggressive instead of frightened, and so competitive that you are unable to relax, you must calm down. Try yoga, deep breathing, biofeedback—anything that enhances your awareness of yourself and gives you some control over your nerves and emotions. As for the show itself, try showing *hors concours*. When you know that you are not competing, you may be able to relax and just ride your horse. Alternatively, take your horse to a show outside your chosen discipline, where you don't expect to win and where you are not up against your usual rivals. A hunter rider might enjoy a schooling dressage show; a dressage rider who enjoys jumping low fences might enjoy a schooling hunter show.

In any case, the point is to change the situation enough so that your own killer competitive instincts aren't aroused. Create a situation where you are *showing* but not *competing*. You can then work your horse calmly, and consciously begin to set up a new set of expectations for yourself. This will give you a chance to learn to focus on how you're *riding*, not on how you're *doing*. Don't let yourself be limited by your own involvement; don't let your performance be limited by your fixation on "results."

Competition Costs

Showing can be extremely expensive and time-consuming. Most working adults can't get to a lot of shows, even if they have the money. And many don't have the money to attend more than a few local shows each year. When your entire disposable income goes to maintain your horse, it isn't easy to pay for entry fees, stabling, hotels, and food. Whatever you can afford, get the most out of it by being *prepared*. Be sure that you and your horse are both ready and fit. Then, if you relax and do your best, showing can be a lot of fun.

More Money than Time

Plan to attend a few shows that will fit in with your schedule, then sit down with your instructor and make a plan. You will want to use your schooling and lesson time to best advantage to prepare yourself and your horse for these competitions. Take your instructor along to coach you, and have a video made of each ride.

More Time than Money

Learn before you go: attend shows as a spectator, as a groom, or as volunteer help. Offer to set fences and rake arenas. Run score sheets between fences and the secretary's tent. And there are other ways to attend competitions and learn from the judges—without having to compete.

Scribing at Dressage Shows

If dressage is your passion, but you can't afford to do a lot of showing, volunteer to scribe for the judge. Scribing can provide you with an invaluable education. In exchange for your time, you will get insights into what the judge is looking for, and you will learn exactly what is behind the comments written on the tests.

But if you do this, take it seriously. The judge watches the riders, gives number scores, and makes comments, but *you* write them down and make them part of the official show records. The judge is trusting you to record those scores and comments accurately and in the proper place (also legibly and spelled correctly).

Guidelines for Scribes

Before you scribe your first show, read a dressage book or the USDF guides. If your spelling is shaky, practice writing out some of the words. When your hands are cold or your eyes are watering from sun or dust, and you are trying to write quickly, neatly, and accurately in a tiny box, you simply don't have time to puzzle out how to spell "rhythm" or "engagement."

The comments you record will mean a great deal to the riders. Many riders read them carefully and keep their tests (if you are also a competitor, you should do this, too). They compare this year's tests to last year's, and this show's test under this judge to their last show under the same judge, to see what they have managed to improve.

Know the tests that you will be scribing, and know what their score sheets look like. You don't have to be able to *ride* the tests, but you are much less likely to make a mistake while scribing if you know what the movements are and what their order is. If the judge makes a mistake— yes, it happens—and forgets to give you a score for a movement, it is up to you to recognize that her next score and comment don't match your next empty box, and to skip ahead to keep up with the judge. When the test is over (or sooner if it is a low-level, simple test with slower, larger movements), you should ask "How did you score that first canter depart?" or whatever the empty box corresponds to.

Judges often use and reuse long words. You don't have to write them out each time if you can use an easily understood abbreviation. For instance, the first time the judge says "lacks impulsion" or "needs more engagement" in a particular test, write out the phrase. After that, "lacks imp" or "needs more eng" will do. Writing "OF" for "on the forehand," "NS" for "not straight," "irr" for "irregular," and "NOB" for "not on the bit" will save a lot of time and help you to keep up with a judge who is generous with her comments.

After the rider has finished the test, the judge will either fill in the collective marks and comments or ask you to do it. Either way, it isn't a time to make conversation. You are there to listen and write, not to speak, comment, converse, or tell the judge little tidbits about the riders or horses entering the arena. The judge doesn't *want* to know that the gray gelding is only two years old or that the bay mare is on bute. She has a specific job to do: she has to judge what she sees during the four or five minutes of the test, and that's it. She may speculate about the rider's training methods—or the horse's general soundness—but she is unlikely to share her speculations with you.

If she frowns and looks distressed or concerned, don't assume that you know why and jump in with a comment about the current horse and rider. She may indeed be wondering whether the black horse is rein-lame—or she may be wondering whether she can survive another ten minutes without (a) coffee or (b) a trip to the bathroom.

Scribe's Packing List

You will need:

>   Sunglasses (for glare and dust)
>
>   Sunscreen
>
>   Facial tissues
>
>   A watch set to official show time
>
>   Clipboard (this holds papers steady and allows you to change your position without interfering with the judge).
>
>   Pencils, extra pencils, and more extra pencils! Mechanical pencils (take spares) are good because you can keep on writing without wearing down the point of your pencil; in the winter when your hands are cold and you aren't as precise about pressure, pencil tips tend to break. Pencils are appropriate for all AHSA dressage tests (to scribe FEI tests you would need pens, not pencils).

Being a Judge's Go-Fer at Hunter Shows

If hunter shows are what you like best, you can sometimes arrange to sit with the judge, especially at smaller, less formal competitions. Hunter show judges don't need scribes: they usually write their own scores, since they aren't expected to give lengthy comments or reasons. They record the contestant's number and then make a mark in each box representing a jump. Each judge uses a particular set of marks indicating good jump, tight legs, loose legs, hanging leg, chipped, stood off, overjumped, refused, ran out, broke the jump into splinters, or whatever.

You can learn a lot by sitting with a hunter judge and listening to her comments. And judges appreciate good go-fers; fetch her coffee or a soft drink, get her sunscreen or tissues, hand off the score sheets to the runners. It will give you a clear idea of what exactly is considered to be a good round, and why. This will give you something to practice at home, and will also let you know whether this sort of competition would suit you and your horse.

Watch and Learn

You can learn from watching riders at any competition. If it isn't in your chosen discipline, go anyway. Watch everyone, and keep an open mind. Riders tend to focus exclusively on the techniques and styles of their own specialties, but we can all learn from others. Event riders tend to be a little bit rough-and-ready; we could benefit from acquiring some of the style and polish found at hunter or dressage shows. Many dressage riders could benefit from observing enthusiastic, energetic event riders and horses. Almost all riders could benefit from learning more about presentation and jogging their horses in hand, and the best way to learn this is by watching a Showmanship class at a western show.

When Things Go Wrong

Things won't always go perfectly; there will be bad days. At some point, you will attend a show where something—or everything—will go wrong. You will be late, the ground will be too hard or too muddy, you will be feeling lousy, your coach will arrive an hour after your ride—or your horse will be "off." Don't let it ruin your day, your week, or your interest in riding or showing. If you are still upset when you get home, think about your motivations and goals. Remember why you wanted to show, and what you wanted out of it. And no matter what happened, remember that your most traumatic experience, your worst ride, and your most embarrassing moment will eventually become your best war stories. Keep it all in perspective, and remember that you do it for fun.

Total Recall

It's not always easy to evaluate the quality of your own ride, especially if you are nervous. If you can manage it, take your coach with you or get someone to tape your rides. It will help you get the most out of the time and money you put into the show. You can improve on your performance much more easily if you know exactly what happened and how it looked, and not just how you think you remember it felt. A videotape of your best ride—or your worst—can be worth much more than a thousand words.

Clinics

Riding in a clinic can be a useful way to improve your skills in an environment less stressful than that of a show. This lets you prepare as though you were going to a show, and ride in front of someone knowledgeable—other than your regular instructor. If you suffer from "competition nerves," make a point of wearing your show clothes and braiding even if the clinic is not meant to be formal. This will give you a chance to associate "show stuff" with a lesson.

Getting the Most from a Clinic

Go to the Right One   When you have found a clinic in your area of riding—dressage, cross-country, or whatever—be sure to sign up for the right level. Follow the guidelines, and be accurate about your horse's experience and your own.

Be Prepared   If you and your horse are both physically fit, you will be able to do what the clinician asks, and you will have a much better time.

Be Well-Turned-Out   You and your horse should look as if you are going to a show, for several reasons: it shows respect for the clinician, it is good practice for you, and it will look better if you have someone taping your ride.

Be Organized   Be sure to bring everything you need, including—with the clinician's permission—someone to videotape your lesson.

Be Ready to Listen   Answer any questions that the clinician asks, but otherwise say as little as possible. You are paying to listen.

Select the Clinician Carefully   Some factors to consider are the individual's area of specialty and reputation. Personal references are helpful—what do people who have ridden with this clinician have to say about him or her? Sometimes it just isn't possible to be so careful: either you don't know the clinician at all or there are very few clinicians who come through your area, so you feel that you must take advantage of whatever comes your way.

When It's Your Turn

Give the clinician the information he/she needs. When you introduce yourself, you can add a line or two to your intro. Not all your goals and dreams—you obviously want to improve your riding and your horse's performance or you wouldn't be riding in a clinic in the first place. Supply a few brief facts about the age and fitness level of your horse. If you are recovering from flu or surgery, or if your horse was in a pasture until last month, say so. If you don't know precisely how to describe the level at which your horse goes, or you ride, don't worry. These are facts that will be instantly apparent to the clinician anyway.

At my clinics, I generally ask riders to come up one by one and introduce themselves and their horses. Here are some typical introductions:

"I'm Maggie Taylor and this is Malta. He's a five-year-old Thoroughbred off the track. I bought him when he was three and turned him out for a year, so we've really just been working together for one year. He's still pretty nervous, so I want to keep things really low-key and quiet. He seems to learn better that way. He still jigs a lot when I want him to walk; I'd like to work on that."

This gives me a specific perspective on horse and rider, and my mind begins to sort through a series of exercises and ideas that might help that particular pair.

"I'm Sarah Carter and this is Liana. She's a nine-year-old Trakehner. She was green when I bought her four years ago and we're showing at First Level now, but she's not doing as well as I think she could be. She's lazy, and when I try to send her forward, she always gets marked 'resistant'."

Again, this would provide me with another perspective on a different horse and rider, and make me think of another series of exercises and ideas.

Your Ride

Once your ride begins, your job is simple: listen to the clinician, do what you're told. Try.

Ride the way you usually do. Especially if you do most of your riding and training alone, you can fall into bad habits. One of the most useful things a clinician can do for you is to point out these habits and suggest things you could do more effectively. It makes it harder for the clinician to help you if you are trying to ride in a special way that you think the clinician wants to see.

If you are riding in a group, watch and listen carefully. Pay attention to the other riders, and observe their difficulties and the clinician's way of dealing with them.

If your clinician offers individual lessons, and you ride alone, *get someone to videotape your lesson.*

Don't leave after your own lesson. Watch as many other lessons as you possibly can.

After your ride, if you have a groom or helper, hand them your horse. Then—even before you take off your boots—sit down somewhere quiet and *take notes on everything you can remember about your ride.* You won't remember as clearly after you've talked to friends and had dinner; write it all down while it's still fresh in your mind.

Clinicians and Instructors

Whether your clinic experience was good, bad, or in between, discuss it with your instructor. If the clinician suggested exercises for you, or advised you to change your position or your tack, discuss these things with your instructor as well. It's important for you to do this, for several reasons. First, it's a courtesy. You and your horse and your instructor are a team. Your instructor will be delighted if you had a good time and disappointed if you didn't. Either way, she will want to know what you did at the clinic, what you worked on, what you learned, and what the clinician's advice was.

Second, whatever changes the clinician may have suggested will have to fit into your overall lesson plan. Some suggestions can probably be incorporated seamlessly, and others may require changing lesson plans and strategy. Either way, your instructor will need to know precisely what was advised, what seemed to work, and what didn't. If your instructor attends the clinic or is familiar with that particular clinician's methods, you will have a built-in advantage. Your instructor will be able to observe and learn what specific techniques the clinician suggests for you; then you, your instructor, and your horse can work together at home.

The clinician is *not* there to blow your regular instructor out of the water. In most cases, what the clinician can and should do is bring a fresh eye and a different set of experiences and ideas to your session. If your preferred clinician and your regular instructor disagree on what your problems are and how they should be solved, you will have to make a choice. If you don't have a regular instructor, then get everything you can from your clinic experience and try to put all the pieces together in a way that will make sense to you and to your horse. Taking notes will help you a lot—and so will that video if you had one made.

Clinic Syndrome

Even if you had the best time of your life at a clinic, keep your perspective. Don't sign up for a different one every weekend. Too many clinics with too many people can be counterproductive—disastrous, even—for your progress and that of your horse. Each individual clinician may have a wonderful, well-thought-out system and get marvelous results from it. But when you attend a clinic, you get a little piece, or a few little pieces, of one particular system.

If you mix and match too many little pieces of too many different systems, the result will be a whole that is much *less* than the sum of its parts. You will be confused and frustrated, your horse will be confused and frustrated, and your instructor will be frustrated (but probably not confused—she'll have seen it before).

As a student, your mission is to watch, listen, learn, and ask questions. In addition to collecting information, you have to learn to sift it, filter it, and evaluate it. Use the best—but be sure that it *is* the best. And remember that your best value for money is probably the time you spend with your own instructor; be sure to discuss new ideas and equipment with her *before* putting them into practice. Riding and training skills are best acquired as part of a sensible, considered package.

What if You Make a Mistake?

Occasionally, you may feel that you have made a mistake in signing up for a particular clinic. This can be awkward, especially if the clinician is someone you know nothing about. What do you do if you suddenly realize that you hate his methods—and you are already in mid-session?

You may certainly avoid or refuse to do anything that is violent or painful—but think about it first. Don't confuse discipline with gratuitous violence. An inexperienced rider told to "see-saw the bit to make the horse get his head down" might not feel that there was anything wrong, but if told to "smack the horse behind the leg with the whip, once, sharply" might feel that this was undue violence. A more experienced and knowledgeable rider would have no problem administering one brief sharp correction, but would quite rightly refuse to see-saw the bit!

Beware the "Quick Fix"

Some clinicians may feel obliged to provide you with a quick cosmetic "fix" for a problem, but you don't have to go along with it. Remember that this sort of "fix" is what many people ask for; some riders don't feel that they have gotten their money's worth from a clinic unless they go home with a formula to use, a trick to play, or a gadget to buy. But you and your horse are a team, and you will still be working together long after the clinician has left town. Don't do anything that would damage or endanger that relationship.

Benefits of Clinics

Part of the joy of working with horses is that you get to use your brain *and* your hands. Whether you have had a physically stressful, mind-numbing day on the factory floor, a mentally exhausting, physically immobile day at a desk, a frustrating misunderstanding with a boss, co-worker, child, or spouse, you can come to the barn and leave it all behind. Working with your horse can help you regain your emotional balance and feel more complete.

You may ride for competitive success, for the acquisition of a physical skill, for the intellectual stimulation of processing new information, or for the joy of communication with horses. Whatever your reason for riding, progress, not perfection, should be your goal. A good clinic can boost your self-esteem and confirm that you, your horse, and your instructor are on the right track.

You have an obligation to become the best rider you can be, and to make your horse the best horse that he can be. When you attend a competition or a clinic, you are trying to improve your riding and your horse's performance. But your approval of yourself, like your approval of your horse, should be conditioned on trying, not on performance. Don't fear failure; failure is honorable. The opposite of success is not failure, it is quitting—or not trying. Whether you are at a show or a clinic, keep your emphasis on effort, not on outcome. You don't have to win, but you should go home satisfied with the effort that you made.

Horse Sense and Horsemanship

Horsemanship means much more than just riding skills, although those are important. Horsemanship combines manners, judgment, values, and equestrian tact. A rider may be able to get on a horse and pilot him successfully around a course, but a horseman can do much more.

To be a horseman is to understand and respect the horse, his body systems and his mind, and to use that understanding and respect to achieve your goals of conditioning and training. The ideas and ideals here are what we, as riders and trainers, should strive to achieve. We won't always succeed, but we shouldn't ever stop trying.

The rules of horsemanship are not a set of formulas and fixes—each horse is unique, each situation is different—but a set of guidelines that offer you a way to approach horses and riding with intelligent understanding. Learning horse sense and horsemanship will provide you with a toolbox so that you can fix things yourself—or, even better, maintain them so that they don't go wrong in the first place.

Give yourself every advantage. Many people begin with no understanding of equine nature and behavior: they have no idea what sort of animals horses are. Without at least a basic understanding of horses and their physiology and psychology, riders will have little or no idea of what they can reasonably expect from their partner in the sport of riding.

Luanne Thulstrup, 41, on-air personality (disc jockey), and her Trakehner mare Zeitig ("Greta").

"Interacting with the animal is my hands-down favorite aspect of having horses in my life. It is a privilege to work and spend time with such noble and delightful creatures. My horse is one of the most charming creatures I've ever encountered. She's a good friend."

Horse Sense:
Understanding the Horse

If you understand how horses and humans are alike, and how they differ, you will avoid a lot of trouble in your dealings with horses. If you understand horses in general, your perceptions of your own horse will be more accurate, and your training and riding will go more smoothly. If you are going to understand your horse well enough to train it kindly and effectively, you will have to learn how a horse thinks.

Horses are herd animals. This can work to our advantage since most horses are followers and are therefore likely to cooperate with us when we want them to do something. Because they are group animals, they are extremely sensitive to the emotions of others. Trying to shout down an emotional horse just won't work—you will simply set up a feedback loop, with both horse and rider getting steadily more agitated. The only way to deal with an agitated, emotional horse is to be very quiet and calm yourself.

Their herd instinct is what makes horses reluctant to leave the barn. It also makes them jump better towards home, or towards the trailers—and it is what makes them run back into a burning barn. Herd instinct tells them that their safety is in the group, that their safety *is* the group. Human management has replaced the herd with the barn; to the domesticated, stall-kept horse, the building *is* the herd.

Horses have basic needs. They require food, water, shelter, company, space, and movement.

Horses think, communicate, and learn—but not in the same way that humans do.

Horses are primarily reactive. Don't look for hidden motives. The better you understand their nature, the more predictable their reactions will be.

Fear

In horses, the fear reaction overrides everything else. No amount of training, conditioning, and genuine affection for his handler will eradicate the fear reaction in a horse.

Flight

Fear gives rise to the flight-or-fight reaction. Flight is always the first choice for a horse—flight means safety. The horse is not a claws-and-jaws predator. His protection is different. The horse has the ability to notice potential danger (that is, anything sudden, loud, or strange) and the ability to get away from it quickly. When he senses danger, his desire is to run.

Fight

The fight reaction occurs only when flight is impossible and the horse is—often literally—backed into a corner with no chance of escape.

Training versus Instinct

We spend much of our time asking horses to do things that go against their instincts. We ask them not to pull back or run away when they are frightened or hurt; we demand that they stand quietly in the presence of a frightening object. Your horse learns by association. And for a horse (but not for a human), association implies causation. If your horse shies at a lawnmower and you beat him for shying, you may think you are teaching him not to shy. But your horse will be forever convinced that lawnmowers are frightening *and* cause pain.

The Natural Horse

The horse is a grazing animal whose physical systems and inclinations would, in nature, keep him walking and eating sixteen to twenty hours each day. He would have lots of low-impact exercise, a low-protein diet, and a low-stress life.

Horses do not naturally perceive food as a reward. Unlike a predator, with a long species history of getting food as the result of personal effort, the horse is a prey animal, hamburger on the hoof—fast food, so to speak.

The horse has no concept whatsoever of getting food as the result of a focused, determined, all-out personal effort. You can teach your horse to enjoy—and expect—treats, but you won't be able to convey the idea that he should work hard now so that he can eat dinner later.

Your horse can't think like a predator; he can't think like a human, either. Your horse can't be taught to understand your point of view. But humans can learn to think like horses, or at least to understand how horses think. If you are willing to make the effort, you can learn to see things from your horse's point of view.

Left to himself, your horse would graze and sleep and roll and play, but he would never practice circles, transitions, or square halts. He wouldn't jump a course of obstacles when he could easily walk around them. Everything you ask your horse to do is *your* idea. And since the whole process of communication is your idea, you should try to learn his language while you teach him some of yours. Your horse can be your partner, your friend, your companion, but he is not a machine, a big dog, or a human being with four legs. You need to understand your horse's natural likes and dislikes, his fears and habits, his love of company, and his need for a predictable environment. You need to know what is natural for your horse so that you won't praise or blame him for being what he is. He is fearful, reactive, and he can't evaluate the morality of a situation. If you are to become a horseman, you must learn to understand your horse's point of view—you must learn to think like a horse.

Why Do You Train Your Horse?

You train so that you can develop your horse into an educated partner so that both of you will enjoy your time together. Training your horse does not mean *forcing* him to submit to your will, but *educating* him to understand what you want and building his body so that he can do it. It means building up his self-confidence so that he believes he can do what you ask. It also means building up his trust in you so that he will believe you if you think he can do it. If your horse believes in you, he will do things he isn't sure about: go across the stream, into the dark woods, past the motorcycle or lawnmower or horse-eating cows, or down the hill and over an unfamiliar cross-country jump.

How Do You Train Your Horse?

If you can work with the horse's mind, his body will follow. If training is reduced to its absolute basic principle, it is this: make the wrong thing difficult, make the right thing pleasant. The right way becomes easy when it is learned and understood and practiced, not when it is forced. Think about the aims of dressage: to create a supple, obedient, balanced horse.

You must have your horse's trust if he is to relax and learn. No training method should ever cause injury or pain. If you keep this in mind at all times, you will save time, effort, and money. You can eliminate a lot of tack and gadgets (including most of the bits in the average bit cabinet), and you won't have to spend time trying to regain your horse's trust after you have hurt him.

Shaping Your Own Behavior

If you are going to shape a horse's behavior, you must first shape your own. You must learn to project calm, quiet authority. You must lead so that your horse can relax and follow. Your horse should regard you as the "alpha horse" in the herd—even if the "herd" consists of two members. Your horse will not resent your dominance, which is simply your leadership, as long as you don't confuse dominance with force or brutality. You can assert yourself as much as you like, as long as your assertiveness means that you are definite, clear, and consistent. If you are firm and clear, and praise your horse whenever possible, he will feel secure. If your horse understands what his job is, and that he is doing what is expected of him and doing it well (that is, pleasing you), he will be contented.

Shaping Your Horse's Behavior

You can train your horse most effectively if you can let him know, clearly and pleasantly, what you want from him. Your horse needs to know what his job is, and that he does it well, and that you are pleased with him.

To do what you want, the horse must

- Understand what you want him to do

- Be physically able to do it

- Be in a position to do it

To get what you want from the horse, you must

- Teach the horse what you want

- Prepare him mentally and physically so that he is able to do what you want

- Put him in the correct position to do it

- Ask clearly for what you want

- Let him know when he has done what you wanted him to do

Encourage or Discourage Behavior

Training is often represented as a system of behavior modification through a system of reward and punishment. I prefer the idea of encouragement and discouragement. Training by this system is a fairly peaceful process: you simply encourage the behaviors you want, and you discourage those you don't want. You want your horse to understand and cooperate, not to obey from fear. In psychological terms, you are performing positive (motivational) shaping to modify your horse's behavior. To achieve your goals, you mold your horse's behavior gradually, rewarding him for the desired behavior. At first, you reward generously and frequently, showing your appreciation for *any* hint of the behavior you want.

Then, as the behavior becomes more established and more precise, you offer rewards less often, and only for better performance. In this way, you shape your horse into the horse you want. This system is based entirely on reward and encouragement. If you don't like a behavior, you simply don't reward it. Ask again for what you wanted, watch for any hint of the desired behavior, and then reward and encourage the behavior you do want. It's basically a binary system, where 1 equals reward, and 0 equals no reaction.

You always give the horse enough time to understand what you want and enough time to respond to your aids. Then, depending on his response, you can either *encourage* the behavior by giving him a pat, a stroke, a kind word—or by ceasing the demand—or *discourage* it by putting him calmly back into position and repeating the sequence of aids. The value of this system lies in the calm it produces in both horse and rider. your horse is encouraged or asked again, but never frightened or threatened: you are teaching him what *to do*, not telling him what *not* to do. And you are able to remain relaxed and positive; you don't *have* to react to everything your horse does.

You must be able to communicate clearly with your
horse, whether you want him to shorten his stride . . .

. . . or lengthen it.

Why Do Horses Obey?

If you are returning to riding after many years away from the sport, or if your early riding experiences were limited to trail rides at summer camp, you may need to change some of your basic ideas about how horses learn and why they do what they do. Most of us can remember long-ago lessons or trail rides, with the adult in charge telling us "If he doesn't do what you want, kick him hard; he knows better" or "Don't let him get away with anything—hit him!" If a horse trotted instead of walking, or walked instead of trotting, or didn't respond "correctly" when his rider began flapping the reins and yelling, the rider was always told to punish the horse.

Many lesson barns operated much the same way. Their "lessons" were, effectively, trail rides without the trail—a group of children on quiet horses that followed each other, nose to tail, around an arena for an hour. There was never any suggestion that the rider could be at fault, or that a horse might have misunderstood. The rider, no matter how inexperienced or inept, was expected to dominate the horse, and that was that. This sort of riding, and this sort of advice from adults who "knew about horses," led many impressionable young-sters to grow up believing that when horses do things wrong, it is because they are "trying to get away with something" or because they are out to get us, and that when they do things right, it is because they fear punishment.

Nothing could be more wrong. Horses respond to positive signals, and they are quick to learn what behaviors please us—if we let them know when we are pleased. A horse would prefer to do whatever is easi-est, and will remember and repeat any behavior that got him something he liked, whether the "something" was a piece of sugar, a pat, a kind word, or—perhaps the best reward of all—peace and quiet: the end of the schooling session.

When you are working with your horse, there is no place for abuse and no place for you to indulge in fits of temper. You are training, which means that you are teaching. Your purpose is to educate your horse, not to intimidate or frighten him. Like a child in school, a horse is most likely to learn if the instructions are given clearly and he is given con-stant encouragement. Hitting or jerking a horse for making a mistake is like slapping or jerking a child because he didn't understand what you were saying or wasn't able to answer correctly or quickly enough to suit you. You may succeed in making him cower, and you may even terrorize him. But you will not be able to force him to learn, and the next time he sees you, he will begin to worry. And a worried horse is a tense horse. What you want is a relaxed horse that will understand your signals and trust you enough that he won't panic whenever he *doesn't* understand something. If he is relaxed and secure, he will be able to learn; if he is relaxed, secure, and physically able to do what you want him to do, you will be able to teach him just about anything.

Slow, Progressive Training

Training is not a quick process. The only way you can save time is by taking time. Each stage of training is based on the previous stages, and the completion of one stage prepares the horse, physically and mentally, for the demands of the next stage. Don't rush—anything you skip or skimp in the early stages will come back to haunt you later. Your horse will learn his lessons well if you combine a progressive, logical, step-by-step program with a thinking and feeling approach to training. There are no shortcuts to correct training; slow and steady is the only way.

A common example of wrong training is a rider pulling a horse's head in towards his chest and forcing it downward by using low, heavy hands or by see-sawing the bit in the horse's mouth. The rider imagines that this will somehow "put the horse on the bit" or "get the horse collected," because she has looked at an upper-level dressage horse and completely misunderstood what she was seeing. Another common example is a trainer who keeps raising the height of jumps to "get the horse's attention" or to "make him figure it out." A horse that jumps too fast or too carelessly over a 3' fence does not need a 4' fence to sharpen him up; he needs to be trained. A well-trained and responsive jumper will clear a single upended barrel—or a single kitchen chair.

Discipline

There *is* a place for discipline in training. You must always be clear about your expectations, and that includes being clear about which of your horse's actions are unacceptable. There are times when a short, sharp smack can be an excellent form of communication—when a horse nips, for instance, and needs to be shown *immediately* that biting is not an acceptable behavior.

Horses discipline each other all the time. Horses brought up outdoors, in mixed-age groups, recognize and respond to older-horse discipline immediately. Watch a mare with a pesky foal: after a point, the kicking and bouncing baby will be met with a maternal ears-back squeal and nip. Sometimes the nip removes hair or a little skin, but there is no doubt that (a) the mare loves her foal and (b) the mare knows how to get her point across. If you discipline your horse quickly and sharply, the way his mother did, you too will get your point across with minimum effort. If your horse was brought up by a tired, tolerant mare, or if he was weaned and sent off to bring himself up with a peer group, you may have your work cut out for you.

Yes, you can discipline your horse. But your discipline should be like horse discipline: deserved, swift, timely, to the point, possibly (briefly) painful, and then over and done with, with no hard feelings, because the point has been made.

Before you discipline your horse, be clear about which behavior you are actually punishing. Then be sure that it is equally clear to your horse. If he lifts his head when you try to bridle him, and you jerk the reins as soon as the bridle is in place, you may believe that you have punished him for putting his head up. Your horse's interpretation of the sequence of events will be quite different: he will be convinced that he was punished for being bridled. If he steps on your foot, which he can't see, and you hit him, he won't "learn to stay off your foot"; he will learn that you are a person who hits for no reason. If he bucks and you smack him on the bottom, hard, while he is bucking, he will associate bucking with the pain and indignity of getting smacked. But if he bucks and you are too busy hanging on to hit him until he has stopped bucking, what will his interpretation be? He may believe that he has been punished for stopping—did you want him to keep on bucking? Or he may feel that you have hit him for no reason and are not to be trusted. In the first case, he will probably buck longer the next time; in the second case, he will be apprehensive about anything you do.

The Three-Second Rule

Whether you are praising or rebuking your horse, use the *three-second rule*: if you are going to encourage or discourage a behavior, do so within three seconds. Otherwise the horse will have gone on to something else, physically and mentally, and won't have a clue why he is being patted or smacked. If you are not dealing with a completely unacceptable behavior, like biting, there is probably no need to punish the horse anyway. But if you feel that you cannot possibly ride or train without the option of punishing, at least try to follow some reasonable guidelines.

If you are absolutely convinced that your horse has deliberately disobeyed a simple command which he understood perfectly and was physically in a position to carry out, *and* if your punishment will follow the disobedience by no more than three seconds, *then* punishment (in the form of one quick, sharp smack to the horse's behind) may be appropriate.

If there is any chance that your horse might have disobeyed out of pain, confusion, fear, or that the command was not perfectly clear, or that the horse was not physically in a position to carry out the command, then punishment is inappropriate. "Letting it go" is always an option— and often the best option. Failure to punish does *not* reinforce the wrong behavior, but inappropriate punishment will create further behavior problems.

Keep your discipline in context. Be sure that you know what the disobedience means. If you know that your horse is physically capable of jumping a particular jump, and you ride him down to it and he stops, be sure that you know what the stop means. Whether your horse needs encouragement or discipline at that moment will depend on whether he was saying "I can't do this" or "I won't do this."

Horses do not, as a rule, trot around smugly saying to themselves "Ha, ha, I got away with THAT, clever clever me, she didn't hit me," but they do, very much, resent undeserved punishment. An upset, confused, or sullen horse is not easy to train or pleasant to ride. Being too lenient is better than being too severe; one of your main goals should be to teach your horse that his time with you is something to enjoy, not to endure. If you give your horse the benefit of the doubt most of the time, he will learn to trust you, and he will reciprocate when you do something inappropriate. Well-treated horses are very forgiving; a horse that has received consistent, tactful handling is resilient enough to bounce back without setbacks or permanent psychic scars if his rider has an occasional lapse or makes an error in judgment.

End-of-Session

The presentation and timing of work can alter your horse's attitude towards it. The last thing you do before stopping work becomes something the horse enjoys—it gives the ultimate reward. *Progress is incremental.* If you are having trouble achieving a particular movement, remember to reward the attempt, not just the perfect performance.

If you are sure that your aids are correct, that the horse understands them, and that there is no physical reason preventing the horse from doing what you want, relax, lengthen your reins, and ask again. Then, if you perceive even the hint of an attempt to do what you want, get off and end the session.

Your horse can learn to do what you ask out of trust or out of fear. With the exception of tricks that involve reaching for food, it is very unlikely that you will be able to incorporate physical and emotional motivation (anything that makes the horse act, or respond) into your training program. Your horse is driven to satisfy his basic physical needs, but it is difficult for a trainer to devise a reward system based on eating, drinking, rolling, and having sex.

Conditioned responses aren't absolutely reliable. As adults, we know exactly what fatigue or distraction can do to our own conditioned responses. We may have driven for twenty years or more, but how many of us have stopped when the light changed to yellow, then—inadvertently, without thinking—started forward again as it turned red? Your horse, too, can be tired, uncomfortable, or distracted, and can make a mistake.

You must reinforce your horse's conditioned responses. All learned skills need reinforcement. If you want a certain conditioned response to become reliable, then practice it. The keys to achieving a reliable response are time, consistency, and repetition.

Old Horses, New Tricks

Don't worry that your horse is "too old" to learn something new. An older horse can learn new responses, and can learn something new, whether you want to begin trail riding, dressage, or driving. As long as that horse is alive and kicking (so to speak), its brain is functioning. There is no point at which the brain shuts down and cannot accept any new information or input. This can work to your advantage if you want to take your seventeen-year-old Saddlebred out of Country Pleasure classes and begin dressage training (a friend of mine did precisely that a few years ago with great success). But this responsiveness to new input can also work to your disadvantage if your new job makes it impossible for you to ride except on weekends, and you assume that your horse is so well-trained that his responses will remain reliable no matter who rides him or how.

Old Training Versus New Input: The Downside

Every year, would-be dressage riders with more money than sense spend huge sums on horses they cannot ride. They assume that the horses will remain at Fifth or Fourth or Third Level until the riders catch up. In fact, the opposite usually occurs. The Fourth Level horse quickly becomes a Third Level horse, then a Second Level horse, then a First Level horse. At some point the rider usually decides that she has been cheated and that the horse wasn't so well-trained after all. She sells him, buys a new one, and the cycle begins again.

Conditioned Learning

Keep the principles of conditioned learning in mind at all times, even when you aren't actively schooling your horse. Be careful what you teach him: don't inadvertently discourage or encourage a behavior by comforting or consoling him at the wrong moment. If you begin your warm-up, he spooks at the barn cat and leaps in the air, and you stop and comfort him, "Poor baby, did the kitty scare you? It's just Mousebreath, he won't hurt you," perhaps patting him as well, don't be too surprised if he spooks the next time you get on or the next time he notices Mousebreath walking through the arena.

Your horse will learn, and will keep learning. Whether he learns what he picks up on his own, what you teach him inadvertently, or what you want him to learn, under your supervision, is up to you.

Morality

Your horse does not consider any behavior to be "right" or "wrong." He can and will learn that certain behaviors will be encouraged, or rewarded, and that others will be discouraged, or punished. But he cannot learn to think of any of these behaviors as "good" or "bad." You can't make your horse feel guilty, so don't try. What you *can* do is make your horse feel apprehensive, which is something else entirely. If he does something he shouldn't and you hit him or yell at him, he may learn to associate what he did—or perhaps merely your presence—with being hit or yelled at, and he may begin to shift about and put his head up and his ears back if the situation arises again, but that is apprehension (Uh-oh, I'm in trouble), not guilt (I have done something that was morally incorrect).

Ask the Right Question

When your horse exhibits a behavior you don't like, especially if it has come on rather suddenly, be sure you are asking yourself the right question. "How do I make him stop this?" is the wrong question. "Why is he doing this?" is the right question. For example, imagine a horse that lands over fences awkwardly, with his head flipping up far too high for the safety of the rider's nose. If you ask "How do I make him stop this?", the answer will probably involve something mechanical, like a tight standing martingale, which will prevent the horse from putting his head so high into the air. But what you really need to know is the cause of the horse's behavior.

If you ask "Why is he doing this?", the answer will involve a process of eliminating possible causes. You will first look into the possibility of physical pain or discomfort as a cause of undesirable behavior. Then you will look at fear, then at lack of understanding—and you will rarely need to go any further.

In this particular case, the answer might be as simple as a badly fitting saddle hurting the horse's back. It might be a reaction to the rider's catching the horse's mouth with the bit after each jump. Or it might be that the horse's front feet hurt, perhaps from bruised soles or from something nastier like navicular, and that he is simply doing his best to land without taking quite so much weight on his front feet. In none of these cases would a standing martingale help the horse, nor would it address the underlying reason for the behavior.

One-Sidedness

Most horses are noticeably one-sided; that is, they take up contact more reliably on one side than another, prefer one trotting diagonal to the other, and move more smoothly on one canter lead than on the other.

Most humans are one-sided as well. We work to overcome the one-sidedness of our horses, often without realizing that we too have a dominant and a non-dominant side. If you know which is your dominant side, or if you don't think you are one-sided, try this exercise: cross your arms, or fold your fingers together, and notice that you always put the same arm, and the same thumb, on top. Try it the other way: it's slower, more awkward, and doesn't feel right. Be aware of your own one-sidedness, and try to overcome it so that you can help your horse overcome his.

Whether you are working your horse on the longe or under saddle, work him in his more difficult direction first. If you become tired, or your schooling session is interrupted, or if you lose track of time and have to finish suddenly, you will already have stretched his tighter side. When you become frustrated with your horse's inability to move equally well in both directions, remember that riders are also one-sided. The difference is that you know about it, you care about it, and you can act to change it. Your horse isn't being "resistant" or uncooperative in one direction; he is just stiff. It's more difficult for him to work that way, and you will have to take that into account as you ride and train.

Boredom in the Horse

You are responsible for your horse's physical and mental well-being. Don't bore your horse. Malnutrition and abuse can damage a horse mentally and physically, but so can boring, monotonous work. Your horse needs variety and an occasional change of outlook. This does not necessarily mean "time off," which usually just means longer turnout time, but it does mean a change from the usual routine. Time spent outdoors is usually appreciated by horses. Your dressage horse would benefit from an occasional trail ride; your show jumper might appreciate a hack out in the country; your hunter might like to go to a forest preserve or park, trot up and down a few hills, and walk through a creek.

Pain = No Gain

All training must take into account the physical ability and physical condition of the horse. This means that you must be aware of your horse's current stage in terms of strength, endurance, and in the development of particular muscles and muscle groups. Training should never go beyond what your horse is capable of doing comfortably at that moment. Think about a ballet dancer in her daily class, or a person in any sort of exercise program; the emphasis should always be on gradual development. Stretching is okay, tearing is not.

This is the point at which the ballet dancer analogy fails: dancers often work either in pain or on the edge of pain, but *that is their own decision*. Horses do not make the decisions about their training; we do. Your horse should never be worked in pain or on the edge of pain. It's wrong, and—if you need a more practical reason—it will sabotage your training program. Working in pain will result, at best, in an uncomfortable and resentful animal. And it is very likely to create resistances that impede all progress, and even—all too often—in further injury, sometimes permanently disabling.

When Are You Training?

Training is something you do whenever you work with your horse. If you are impatient and in a hurry one night and try to force the bridle onto his head, and he backs off, you are training him to be head-shy and hard to bridle. If you are so tired you can barely stay upright at the end of a schooling session, and your horse does something wrong just as you are about to dismount, put your foot back in that stirrup, sit up, take a deep breath, and ask that horse for something simple that he does very well. When he does it, pat him and end the session at that moment. You are always training, even if you aren't consciously schooling.

Communication

A rider who is also a horseman is a partner, not just a passenger. And to a rider who is also a horseman, the horse is a partner, not a slave or a piece of equipment. A horseman's goal is cooperation, not coercion; communication, not mere control. The essence of good horsemanship is constant, uninterrupted communication between horse and rider. And that communication is definitely two-way: a dialogue between the rider and the horse, not just a monologue on the part of the rider. Such communication demands great concentration and focus on the part of the rider. It also demands that the rider constantly strive to improve and refine the communication and to lengthen the horse's attention span.

Most of us have seen what happens when people don't speak one another's language. We wince when we see someone getting steadily louder and ruder, apparently convinced that the other person will understand English eventually if the words are spoken loudly enough and often enough. But repetition and loudness will not help; neither will the belief that we are dealing with a stupid individual. If we are going to communicate effectively, we need to do it differently.

But why should you have to make the effort to establish and maintain the process of communication? There are several reasons. For one, it is much easier for you to learn the horse's language than it is for him to learn yours. For another, it is your obligation because the idea was yours in the first place. And finally, the nature of the relationship between you and your horse means that *you* are the leader.

Your horse isn't ambitious, isn't a perfectionist, would never consider doing a perfect straight line, a round circle, a balanced half-pass; your horse has, in short, none of the reasons you do for wanting to do things in a certain way. Your horse wants to be comfortable and at ease; failing that, he wants to be less uncomfortable; failing that, he wants to avoid pain. Your horse wants, very much, not to be frightened, and will go to great lengths to get away from a frightening object or out of a frightening situation. He understands discipline quite well, as long as it is clear, sharp, quick, and happens within three seconds of the action that prompted you to discipline him. He does *not* understand punishment for failing to achieve a desired quality of movement.

Just Say "Yes"

You must reward effort. Set your horse up to succeed, then praise him for trying—keep saying "yes" to him. (You can say "no" instead, but that is negative motivation; you are asking your horse to cooperate in order to avoid discomfort, pain, and fear.) Your horse has only one possible positive motivation for work: enjoyment of your company. And he can only enjoy your company if you (a) don't cause pain and (b) don't cause confusion. A physically comfortable horse that understands what you expect, and perceives you to be pleased with what he does, will be an emotionally comfortable horse as well.

Don't Personalize Conflict

If you have a conflict with your horse, don't personalize it. The horse is not your adversary unless you back him into a corner and convince him that he has no way to please you and no possibility of flight. If your horse has done something you don't like, ask the right question: "What has caused this behavior?", not "Why is he doing this to me?"

Beware of attributing human thought patterns and motivations to your horse; it's unfair to him and won't help your training program. Ascribing planned purposeful behavior to the horse is one of the hallmarks of a bad trainer. Don't allow yourself to make that mistake. If you find yourself thinking that the horse is manipulating you (for instance, faking lameness) or resisting just to be "ornery"; if you find yourself saying "He's really pushing me, but I'm not going to let him get away with it," dismount immediately, put your horse away, and go somewhere else until your perspective has been restored. Stop before your temper comes into play and you ruin what was left of a working relationship.

If your horse has done something that frightened you, breathe deeply and bring yourself back to a calmer state. Our adrenaline prompts us to quick, violent action, but it is not appropriate or useful to hit a horse in anger. If you slap a child who runs out into the street and almost gets hit by a car, you can explain or at least apologize to the child. The child may understand and forgive; your horse will not.

Common Training Errors

Two of the most common errors in training involve the use of two things that have no place around horses.

One is temper—don't use it. Ever.

The other is the temptation to do something wrong to get a result. Don't use incorrect technique or position, even on a very young or green horse. Take your time, use repetition and consistency, be understanding and be clear.

You have to work with what you've got. Luckily for you, you have a lot to work with. First, there are your attributes as an adult rider:

Horsemanship means understanding and appreciating the animals we are privileged to teach and train.

intelligence, determination, communication skills, judgment, patience, and the ability to set and reset your goals. Then there are your horse's attributes: memory, perception, sensitivity, honesty, a willingness to work, and a desire to please. These attributes, together with the tools in your "training toolbox," will enable you to go as far as your resources and ambitions will take you:

> Patience
>
> Humility
>
> Tact
>
> Good communication skills
>
> Good management skills
>
> An understanding of horse physiology and psychology
>
> Respect and affection for horses as a species, and for your horse as an individual
>
> Consistency
>
> Responsibility
>
> Realistic expectations
>
> A clear understanding of cause and effect (and which is which)

Keep Making Sense

Most of the mistakes that people make with their horses result from a lack of understanding. People who don't understand horses tend to project human qualities onto their horses, and therefore have unrealistic expectations, inappropriate reactions, and unsuitable ideas of what constitutes reward and punishment. They misinterpret the signals coming from their horses, then mishandle the horses based on their lack of understanding.

You must teach and train a horse in a way that makes sense to the horse in horse terms, not in a way that would make sense to a person in a horse suit. The more you understand horses in general and your horse in particular, the more you will be able to reason backwards from effect to cause, and the more effective your training will be. If you can take the principles of progressive training and apply them in a quiet, calm atmosphere, and build on success by using the tools just listed, you will be using horse sense and horsemanship for the benefit of your horse and yourself.

Books and Tapes

Books and tapes are wonderful training tools, but unless you have both unlimited financial resources and shelf space, you will have to shop selectively.

Books Own as many good ones as you can afford. Buy books that you will want to read or refer to again and again: the classic reference works and your own personal favorites.

Make good use of your local library. Most libraries have some books on horses and riding, and you aren't limited to your own library's collection. Through the interlibrary loan service, you can get books from other libraries around the country.

Videos Videos are costly, but you may not need to purchase them in order to view them. Horse videos are rarely available through the library system, but many tack stores have videos for rent, and there are several video clubs and services that rent riding and training videos. This gives you a chance to try before you buy.

When you find a video you want to own, you may be able to share the cost with other like-minded people. Ask your riding instructor (riding instructors are often a good source of videos), your fellow students, or boarders at your barn.

Audio Cassettes   If your only free time is your driving time, audio tapes give you a chance to learn uninterrupted.

Here is a very short list of items that I feel are especially helpful to riders who do most of their schooling alone.

Books

Self-Awareness

Hassler, Jill. *In Search of Your Image.* Missoula, Mont.: Mountain Press Publishing Company, 1993. Also the accompanying workbook.

Savoie, Jane. *That Winning Feeling!* North Pomfret, Vt.: Trafalgar Square Publishing, 1992.

Rider Fitness

Holderness-Roddam, Jane. *Fitness for Horse and Rider.* North Pomfret, Vt.: Trafalgar Square Publishing, 1993.

Meyners, Eckart. *Fit for Riding.* Boonsboro, Md.: Half Halt Press, Inc., 1992.

Conformation and Movement

Bennett, Deb. *Principles of Conformation Analysis, Vols. 1–3.* Gaithersburg, Md.: Equus Collection, 1989.

Harris, Susan E. *Horse Gaits, Balance and Movement.* New York: Howell Book House, 1993.

Oliver, Robert, and Bob Langrish. *A Photographic Guide to Conformation.* London: J. A. Allen, 1991.

Thelwall, Jane. *The Less-than-Perfect Horse.* Distributed by Breakthrough Publications, Ossining, N.Y.: 1993.

Tack and Equipment

McBane, Susan. *The Illustrated Guide to Horse Tack.* North Pomfret, Vt.: Trafalgar Square Publishing, 1992.

Strickland, Charlene. *Tack Buyer's Guide*. Ossining, N.Y.: Breakthrough Publications, 1988.

Working Alone

Haas, Jessie. *Safe Horse, Safe Rider*. Pownal, Vt.: Garden Way Publishing, 1994.

Harris, Susan E. *The United States Pony Club Manual of Horsemanship*. New York: Howell Book House, 1994.

———.*Basics for Beginners/D Level*. New York: Howell Book House, 1994.

———.*Intermediate Horsemanship/C Level*. New York: Howell Book House, 1995.

———.*Advanced Horsemanship/B/HA/A Levels*. New York: Howell Book House, 1996.

Hill, Cherry. *Becoming an Effective Rider*. Pownal, Vt.: Garden Way Publishing, 1991.

Kidd, Jane. *Practical Dressage*. New York: Howell Book House, 1994.

O'Connor, Sally. *Common Sense Dressage*. Boonsboro, Md.: Half Halt Press, Inc., 1992.

Swift, Sally. *Centered Riding*. New York: St. Martin's Press, 1985.

Wallace, Jane. *Flatwork Exercises: Threshold Book # 23*. Boonsboro, Md.: Half Halt Press, Inc., 1994.

Horse Health and Fitness

Giffen, James M., and Tom Gore. *Horse Owner's Veterinary Handbook*. New York: Howell Book House, 1989.

Kellon, Eleanor. *Dr. Kellon's Guide to First Aid for Horses*. Ossining, N.Y.: Breakthrough Publications, 1993.

———. *The Older Horse*. Ossining, N.Y.: Breakthrough Publications, 1986.

Loving, Nancy. *Veterinary Manual for the Performance Horse*. Grand Prairie, Tex.: Equine Research, Inc., 1993.

Meagher, Jack. *Beating Muscle Injuries in Horses*. Hamilton, Mass.: Hamilton Horse Associates, 1985.

Rooney, James. *The Lame Horse*. Ossining N.Y.: Breakthrough Publications, 1992 (reprinted).

Competition

Harris, Susan E. *Grooming to Win*. 2d ed. New York: Howell Book House, 1991.

Hill, Cherry. *From the Center of the Ring: An Inside View of Horse Competitions*. Pownal, Vt.: Garden Way Publishing, 1988.

Morris, George. *Hunter Seat Equitation*. New York: Doubleday, 1989.

Strickland, Charlene. *Show Grooming: The Look of a Winner*. Ossining, N.Y.: Breakthrough Publications, 1986.

Tait, Blythe. *Eventing Insights*. Boonsboro, Md.: Half Halt Press, Inc., 1988.

White-Mullin, Anna Jane. *Winning: A Training and Showing Guide for Hunter Seat Riders*. North Pomfret, Vt.: Trafalgar Square Publishing, 1992.

Trailering

Hawkins Guide staff. *Hawkins Guide to Horse Trailering on the Road*. Southern Pines, N.C.: Blue Green Publishing, Inc., 1995.

Longanecker, Diane. *Trailer-Loading Success*. Yakima, Wash.: Roustabout, 1993.

Legal Matters

Marder, Sue Ellen. *Legal Forms, Contracts & Advice for Horse Owners*. Ossining, N.Y.: Breakthrough Publications, 1991.

Katz, Gary R. *The Equine Legal Handbook*. Boonsboro, Md.: Half Halt Press, Inc., 1993.

Videos (VHS)

Bennett, Deb. *Dr. Deb Bennett's Secrets of Conformation*. Humble, Tex.: Horseman Video, 1993.

Gawhyler, Max. *The Competitive Edge: Improving Your Scores in the Lower Levels*. Columbia, Conn.: Cloverlea Dressage Videotapes, 1994.

Savoie, Jane. *The Half-Halt Demystified, I: Learning the Half Halt*. North Pomfret, Vt.: Trafalgar Square Publishing, 1993.

————. *The Half-Halt Demystified, II: Putting Your Horse on the Bit*. North Pomfret, Vt.: Trafalgar Square Publishing, 1993.

Spencer, Nancy. *Basic Equine Stretching—1994 (second) Edition*. Fairfax Station, Va.: Equitonics, 1994.

Swift, Sally. *Centered Riding, Part I*. North Pomfret, Vt.: Trafalgar Square Publishing, 1985.

————. *Centered Riding, Part II*. North Pomfret, Vt.: Trafalgar Square Publishing, 1986.

Audio Cassettes

Ransehousen, Jessica. *The AHSA Dressage Tests on Cassette*. Steamboat Springs, Colo.: Sasak Enterprises, 1995.

Savoie, Jane. *That Winning Feeling!: Tape 1: Choose Your Future*. North Pomfret, Vt.: Trafalgar Square Publishing, 1993.

————. *That Winning Feeling!: Tape 2: Learning Relaxation and Imaging Skills*. North Pomfret, Vt.: Trafalgar Square Publishing, 1993.

B

Instructor Programs Offering Certification

The following programs offer certification to riding instructors. Please contact them directly if you would like more information about their programs.

American Riding Instructor Certification Program (ARICP)
P.O. Box 282
Alton Bay, NH 03810
(603) 875-4000

The ARICP offers instructor certification in a number of specialties, including hunt seat, dressage, and combined training. It offers the following levels of certification: Instructor in Training (IT), Instructor of Beginner through Intermediate (IBI), Instructor of Beginner through Advanced (IBA), Expert Instructor (EI), and Master Instructor (MI).

The MI is a title that is awarded to specific individuals based on their achievements.

United States Dressage Federation (USDF)
P.O. Box 6669
Lincoln, NE 68506-0669
(404) 434-8550

The USDF offers a dressage instructor certification program, educational programs, regional seminars for instructors, and pre-certification programs.

> CHA/Association for Horsemanship Safety and Education
> 5318 Old Bullard Road
> Tyler, TX 75703
> (800) 399-0138

The focus of this organization (formerly called the Camp Horsemanship Association, hence the CHA in the title) is on safety in group riding programs. They offer a four-level certification program in English and Western riding; candidates may become certified in either or both forms.

Certification clinics, of which there are more than eighty annually in North America, last from four to five days. There are over sixty approved clinic sites in the United States and Canada, and there are additional sites in Australia (CHA certification is valid in Australia, which uses the same standards and manuals; Australian certification is valid in North America).

CHA/Association for Horsemanship Safety and Education and NARHA (North American Riding for the Handicapped Association, Inc.) are working together to create a joint certification program.

> British Horse Society (BHS)
> British Equestrian Centre
> Stoneleigh
> Warwickshire CV8 2LR
> England

The BHS offers a number of certification programs. Among the certificates issued by the BHS are the Assistant Instructor (BHSAI), the Intermediate Instructor (BHSII), the Instructor (BHSI), and the Fellow of the British Horse Society (FBHS).

> United States Combined Training Association (USCTA)
> P.O. Box 2247
> Leesburg, VA 22075
> (703) 779-0440

The United States Combined Training Association (USCTA) does not offer instructor certification, but does maintain a geographically arranged list of combined training and eventing coaches and trainers. The list provides useful information about these instructors, the type and size of their facilities, their student capacity and requirements, their memberships and affiliations, and their professional credentials.

Reliable Mail-Order Sources

Tack/Equipment/Clothing

B.T. Crump Company
1215 East Main Street
Richmond, VA 23219
(800) 282-7867

English saddles and strap goods: equipment for riding, racing, and driving. Horse and rider clothing, stable and health care items.

Back in the Saddle
570-C Turner Drive
Durango, CO 81301
(800) 435-3633

Equipment, clothing, gifts, and books for adults and children. Many unusual toys.

Beval Ltd.
Park Avenue
Gladstone, NJ 07934
(800) 524-0136

English tack, clothing, boots, jewelry, and gifts.

Dover Saddlery
P.O. Box 5837
Holliston, MA 01746
(800) 989-1500

English saddles, tack, equipment, horse and rider clothing, stable and health care items, books, videos, gifts. Large selection of items for ponies and child riders.

Dressage Extensions
27501 Cumberland Road
Bear Valley Springs, CA 93561
(800) 541-3708

Wide selection of dressage saddlery, tack, longeing equipment; also rider clothing, boots, jewelry. A wide selection of dressage books and videos.

Equestrian Enterprise
3011 Trickum Road
Woodstock, GA 30188
(800) 767-1452

Gifts and novelty items and clothing; gold and costume jewelry, watches, etc.

Hartmeyer Saddlery
7111 W. Bethel Avenue
Muncie, IN 47304
(800) 225-5519

Tack, apparel, and equipment for saddleseat and huntseat.

H. Kauffman & Sons Saddlery
419 Park Avenue South
New York City, NY 10016
(800) 872-6687

Their motto is "Everything for the horse and rider since 1875"—tack, apparel, and equipment for all styles of riding.

Libertyville Saddle Shop
P.O. Box M
Libertyville, IL 60048-4913
(800) 871-3353

English and Western saddlery, tack, equipment, clothing, and gifts.

Miller's
235 Murray Hill Parkway
East Rutherford, NJ 07073
(800) 553-7655

English saddles, tack, equipment, horse and rider clothing, stable and health care items, books, videos, gifts. Large selection of items for ponies and child riders.

Ortho-Flex Saddle Co.
Rt. 2, Box 132
Nevada, MO 64772
(417) 667-7834

English, Western, and pack saddles featuring the unique Ortho-Flex panels, which change shape as the horse moves.

Pard's Western Shop, Inc.
306 N. Maple Street
Urbana, IL 61801
(800) 334-5726

Western saddles, tack, equipment, horse and rider clothing, stable and health care items, books, videos, gifts.

Paul's Harness Shop
4255 Sinton Road
Colorado Springs, CO 80907
(800) 733-1223

Prompt, reliable, exceptional service and quality. Top-quality affordable leather halters and girths made in-house. Personal shopper's service: call 1-800-733-1223.

Riding Right, Inc.
Kardas Road
Valley Falls, NY 12185
(800) 545-7444

Special products, many unavailable elsewhere. Custom and semi-custom riding breeches and coats, including maternity breeches.

Schneiders Saddlery
8255 E. Washington St.
Chagrin Falls, OH 44023
(800) 365-1311

Western and English saddlery, tack, equipment, horse and rider clothing, and gifts. Frequent Buyer Bonus Program: purchases earn credit toward a bonus buck certificate.

Tack in the Box
2413 82nd Ave., S.E.
Salem, OR 97301
(800) 456-8225

Tack, equipment, clothing, stable supplies, books, gifts; emphasis on dressage. Special pads, bits, longeing equipment.

Top Tack Inc.
802 Hillman Rd.
Yakima, WA 98908
(509) 966-2090

Tack, equipment, clothing, stable supplies, books, gifts; emphasis on dressage. Special pads, bits, longeing equipment.

Whip 'n' Spur Tack Shop
5055 Van Dyke Road
Lutz, FL 33549-4899
(800) 944-7677

English saddles, tack, equipment, horse and rider clothing, stable and health care items, books, videos, gifts.

Wiese Equine Supply
P.O. Box 192
Eldon, MO 65026-0192
(800) 869-4373

English and Western saddles, tack, equipment, horse and rider clothing, racing tack, stable and health care items, books, videos, gifts.

Discount Tack and Apparel

Chick's
P.O. Box Drawer 59
Dept. 538
Harrington, DE 19952
(800) 444-2441

Discount catalog of horse and rider products for riding and driving.

Grade I Products
299 Hempstead Turnpike
Elmont, NY 11003
(800) 873-8225

Discount catalog of horse and rider products for racing, riding, polo.

State Line Tack
P.O. Box 1217
Dept. HS019
Plaistow, NH 03865
(800) 228-9208

Discount tack, saddlery, equipment, horse and rider clothing, videos, and books.

Custom Boots

E. Vogel, Inc.
19 Howard St.
New York, NY 10013
(212) 925-2460

The Dehner Company, Inc.
3614 Martha Street
Omaha, NE 68105
(402) 342-7788

In-Stock and Custom Blankets

Wilsun Custom Horse Blankets
2210 McFarland/400 Blvd.
Alpharetta, GA 30201
(401) 751-9343 (catalog)

Horse Health Supplies

Horse Health USA
2800 Leemont Ave., N.W.
P.O. Box 9101
Canton, OH 44711-9101
(800) 321-0235

Also carries some English and western saddlery, tack, horse and rider clothing.

Omaha Vaccine Company
First Place Catalog
P.O. Box 7228
Omaha, NE 68107
(800) 367-4444

Also carries some English and western saddlery, tack, horse and rider clothing.

Springtime Feed Co.
10942-J Beaver Dam Road
Cockeysville, MD 21030
(800) 521-3212

Natural remedies and herbal extracts for horses, dogs, and people.

United Vet Equine
14101 West 62nd Street
Eden Prairie, MN 55346
(800) 328-6652

Also carries English and western saddlery, tack, horse and rider clothing, toys.

Valley Vet Supply, Equine Edition
East Highway 36
P.O. Box 504
Marysville, KS 66508-0504
(800) 356-1005

Also carries English and western saddlery, tack, horse and rider clothing, toys.

Specialty Items

Polarfleece riding tights, vests, headbands and ear warmers:

Helmet Helpers, Ltd.
39 Depot Street
Merrimac, NH 03054-3427
(800) 229-5247 for dealer info

Body protector vest:

Tipperary Sport Products
247 Tenth St.
Niagara Falls, NY 14303
(519) 941-7448

Maternity riding breeches:

Riding Right
Kardas Road
Valley Falls, NY 12185
(800) 545-RIGHT

Large-size riding breeches and other clothing:

> 1824
> Arnott Mason Corporation
> P.O. Box 293
> Clifton, VA 22024
> (703) 425-1243

Saddle restuffing:

> The Saddle Shop
> 5008 East Speedway
> Tucson, AZ 85712
> (602) 325-3996

D

Useful Addresses

American Horse Council
1700 K Street, N.W., Suite 300
Washington, DC 20006
(202) 296-4031

American Horse Protection Association
1000 29th St., N.W., #T-100
Washington, DC 20007
(202) 965-0500

American Horse Shows Association
220 E. 42nd St, Suite 409
New York, NY 10017-5809
(212) 972-2472

Hooved Animal Humane Society (HAHS)
P.O. Box 400
Woodstock, IL 60098
(815) 337-5563

Kentucky Horse Park
4089 Iron Works Pike
Lexington, KY 40511
(606) 233-4303

NAHRA (North American Riding for the Handicapped
    Association)
P.O. Box 33150
Denver, CO 80233
(800) 369-7433

Index

Page numbers in *italics* refer to photographs

F

Failure, 3, 21, 23, 194
Farrier, 160
Fear, 5, 51
    Emotional, 6
    Mental, 5
    Physical, 5
First-aid kit
    In the barn, 166–68
    On the road, 168
Fitness, 15, 24, 28, 101
    Aerobic, 28, 31
    As rider protection, 27
    Balance, 30
    Cooling down, 32
    Endurance, 28
    Exercise program, 29, 30
    Exercise equipment, 30
    Flexibility, 28, 31, 32
    Forms of, 28
    Health club, 30
    Injuries, 5
    Resistance training, 29, 30, 31
    Riding muscles, 29, *30*
    Safety, 27
    Strength, 28
    Stretching, 33, 60
    Warming up, 32
    Wear and tear, 5
    Weight and, 38
Fitness program, 39
    Bone, 39
    Muscles, 39
    Tendons and ligaments, 39
Flexibility. *See* Stretching

G

Goals, *14*, 101, 112, 116, 143, 154–55
    Attainable, 19
    Basic, 20

Changing, 19, 23
Competitive, 20
Goal setting, 17, 23
Intermediate, 18
Long-term, 18
Manageable, 22
Personal, 20
Review of, 21
Riding, 20
Short-term, 18
Grooming, 159

H

Health care, 157–73
    Asking questions, 160
    Bleeding, 162
    Colic, 161, 172
    Depression, 161
    Emergency vet care, 162
    Euthanasia, 172–73
    First-aid kit in the barn, 166–68
    First-aid kit on the road, 168
    Grooming, 159
    Horse's appearance, 157
    Medical supplies, 169
    Nutrition, 158
    Pain, 161
    Prevention, 160
    Professional competence, 161
    Professional help, 159–61
    Quick checklist, 157
    Recordkeeping, 170–72
    Telephone procedure, 162–64
    TPR, 162
    Working with your veterinarian, 165
Helmets, 2, 11, 38, 49, 134, 152
Hooved Animal Humane Society
    (HAHS), 104
Horse
    Apprehension, 209
    Attention span, 211